Helping Kids Live Mindfully

Helping Kids Live Mindfully

A Grab Bag of Classroom Activities for Middle School Students

Catherine DePino

ROWMAN & LITTLEFIELD
Lanham • Boulder • New York • London

Published by Rowman & Littlefield
A wholly owned subsidiary of The Rowman & Littlefield Publishing Group, Inc.
4501 Forbes Boulevard, Suite 200, Lanham, Maryland 20706
www.rowman.com

Unit A, Whitacre Mews, 26-34 Stannary Street, London SE11 4AB

British Library Cataloguing in Publication Information Available

Library of Congress Cataloging-in-Publication Data

Library of Congress Cataloging-in-Publication Data Available

ISBN 978-1-4758-3529-8 (cloth : alk. paper)
ISBN 978-1-4758-3530-4 (pbk. : alk. paper)
ISBN 978-1-4758-3531-1 (electronic)

♾ ™ The paper used in this publication meets the minimum requirements of American
National Standard for Information Sciences Permanence of Paper for Printed Library
Materials, ANSI/NISO Z39.48-1992.

Printed in the United States of America

For my granddaughter, Hope Caterina:
Your kind, caring ways
endear you to everyone
you meet along the way.
Family and friends
feel loved when you're
with them because
no matter how busy you are,
you always make time
to be in the moment
with those
you care about most.
Love,
Nonna

Contents

Acknowledgments

I'd like to thank Carlie Wall, associate editor, for her help, kindness, and promptness in responding, and to Emily Tuttle, my acquisitions editor. I also appreciate all the help Caitlin Bean, my production editor, gave me. Thanks to Dr. Tom Koerner, a brilliant force in the publishing industry, for his constant support and encouragement. I greatly appreciate the excellent instruction I received with Robin Boudette, PhD, in the Mindfulness course offered by Jefferson-Myrna Brind Center of Integrative Medicine in Philadelphia, Pennsylvania.

Introduction

How to Use This Book

NOTE TO TEACHERS

You can use this book as part of a mindfulness program in classrooms and can also incorporate it in your lesson plans for regular classes. Additionally, you can use many of the techniques in cooperative learning sessions related to any subject matter to build communication skills and reinforce self-reliance, self-confidence, compassion, and empathy.

Many of the activities complement English/language arts classes as they boost skills in listening, speaking, and writing. You can also use the lessons in social studies and health classes. However you choose to implement the program in your school, the class can discuss their individual experiences practicing Mindfulness in large-group discussions, and small groups can report back to the class about their experiences with the various mindfulness activities. Students can also work as individuals by writing in their Mindfulness Journals and doing home projects related to what they learn in school.

Students can do the mini meditations in class or at home, whatever fits best into your schedule. You may want to use the mini meditations in class after a group activity or a classroom discussion related to Mindfulness. The first part of each meditation asks students to breathe deeply and relax. Advise them to breath in through their noses and out through their mouths. If they want to add an extra breath or two to help them relax, they may. The meditation section also gives students questions to think about related to each section of the book. The actual meditation that students will say silently or aloud is written in italics. Students can say the speaking parts of the mini meditations aloud or in their minds if they do them at home. At school, they will say them silently. Be sure to point out to students that all the speaking parts in the meditations are shown in italics.

The book is called *a grab bag of activities* because after teaching the first two lessons you can turn to any lessons in the book, in any order you want. They will all lead to the same place: a better grasp and appreciation of Mindfulness for your students. As Jon Kabat-Zinn says in his eponymous book, "Wherever you go, there you are."

NOTE TO SCHOOL COUNSELORS AND THERAPISTS

You can use many of the principles and activities in this book in small-group and individual counseling sessions. The "Try It Out" sections, keyed to each topic, provide opportunities in therapeutic settings for discussing the mindfulness principles covered in the book.

Although the mindfulness techniques outlined in this book address the general school population, many of them will assist you with students who present more challenging problems in the areas of relationships with parents, siblings, and teachers, in addition to school issues, anger issues, and problems relating to peers.

NOTE TO KIDS READING THIS BOOK

When your teacher calls the roll, you probably raise your hand and shout out, "Present," but are you really present or just going through the motions?

What would it be like if you could shout out, "Present," not only in school but also everywhere, and live each moment to the fullest as it happens? *Helping Kids Live Mindfully* will take you on an adventure into Mindfulness, a new way of thinking, talking, listening, and relating to all the people in your life.

Mindfulness became popular through the teachings of Dr. Jon Kabat-Zinn, a professor of medicine at the University of Massachusetts. He studied with Buddhist teachers, such as Thich Nhat Hanh, and developed a program to help people improve the quality of their lives by learning techniques that would help them relax and focus. However, Mindfulness is not based on any religion. Rather, it's a way to help you lead a happier and more enjoyable life by staying with the present moment.

If you study and practice the ideas in this book, you'll learn new techniques to help you communicate easily and effectively with everyone in your life. You'll find yourself arguing less with your parents and siblings, enjoying your friendships more, and finding school work less of a hassle.

Best of all, you'll feel more peaceful and able to cope better with any problems that come your way. As a bonus, you'll feel more self-confident and positive about everything. You'll gain a new appreciation for all the people in your life and show more kindness and compassion to everyone. Do you think it seems too good to be true? Try it and see what happens.

Each activity in this book gives you mindfulness techniques to help you deal with many issues that impact your life, such as parents, school, and coping with everyday problems, like moodiness, frustration, and anger. *Helping Kids Live Mindfully* also helps you pack the most enjoyment into everything you do because you're living in the moment rather than in the past or future.

All of the activities in the book have the same format to help make learning Mindfulness easier. First, in each chapter you'll see a brief explanation of the topic called "Be Present" that explains how you can practice Mindfulness effortlessly every day.

The next section, "Try It Out," asks you to take what you've learned out into the world and see how the benefits you gain from living in the present can improve your life. Keep a notebook by your side when you work on this section. You can call it your Mindfulness Journal and decorate it with your own personal touches. If you'd prefer, type your answers on a computer, and save the file to refer to when you want to measure your progress in this mindfulness program. You may want to print out your notes and save them in a folder for easy reference.

As you write brief answers to the questions and do the activities by yourself or with your classmates, it will help you chart your progress in using Mindfulness. If something doesn't work out the way you want it to, try a different approach next time. Mindfulness is a very relaxed process and calls on you to be flexible and follow your intuition, so feel free to experiment with the exercises.

Each segment ends with a mini meditation that reinforces the main points you need to know to practice Mindfulness as effortlessly as it's meant to be. You can do the meditation as part of your school program or at home. The first part of the meditation asks you to completely relax and think about how Mindfulness can help you with different issues that come up in your life that this book mentions. When you do the breathing, breathe in through your nose and out through your mouth. If it would help you relax better, take one or two additional deep breaths.

The second part features the actual meditation, which you can say silently or aloud. You will see the speaking parts for all the meditations printed in italics. You can say the speaking section in your mind when you are in school and silently or aloud when you're at home, whichever makes you the most comfortable. Whether you say it aloud or silently, read the meditation with as much mindfulness as you can muster.

I hope you enjoy learning about Mindfulness and that you'll consider making it part of your life.

NOTE TO PARENTS AND GUARDIANS

Helping Kids Live Mindfully helps middle school children learn the basic principles of Mindfulness. Mindfulness techniques will help your child ground himself in the present moment and will enhance his appreciation of a more peaceful and conflict-free life at home, at school, and when he's with friends. Learning about Mindfulness yourself will enhance your child's experience with Mindfulness. Some activities ask you and other family members to participate. Once you learn about the program, you may want to try some of the techniques at home and at work.

Mindfulness will help your child learn how to talk and listen better and will boost enjoyment of all her activities. Additionally, it will relieve stress, heighten self-confidence, and help her cope with the demands of school and a social life that often seem more complex than in previous generations.

Meditation is an important part of the Mindfulness program. The mini meditations at the end of each lesson will help your child think about Mindfulness in relation to issues that may come up in his life; it also gives him a sense of what it's like to meditate. The first part of the meditation starts with deep breathing and relaxation. It then asks your child to think about how Mindfulness can help with the specific topics addressed in each section of the book. The part that is written in italics is the actual meditation. He can say the parts of the meditations printed in italics silently or aloud if he does them at home. In school, students will read meditations silently.

You may want to go further by teaching your child a simple meditation method and see if she wants to make it part of her daily routine to help her become more mindful and reduce stress. You can find many books and online tutorials about different forms of meditation. If your child would like to delve further into meditation, you can decide together on the type of practice.

Chapter One

Start Living in the Now

BE PRESENT

When you're doing something (eating, taking a shower, playing sports, or cleaning your room), do you find yourself thinking about what you're going to do tomorrow or next week? Maybe you're spending time in the past, thinking of something you did that you wish you'd done differently or thinking how you don't want to make the same mistake again.

Think of what it would be like if you thought mainly about what you're doing in this moment while you're doing it. You'd never miss out on anything because you'd be truly living each moment as you're going through it. And you'd enjoy it more in the process. If you live in the present, everything will appear brighter and more alive to you: the smell and taste of food, the time you spend with friends, and the sight of things you see every day in nature, like the sun, the bright, blooming flowers, and the pinkish-purple sunset.

It's easy to be in the moment if you don't try too hard. Just focus your attention on what's going on right now and be willing to accept it. You'll start to see things in a different way because you're fully present and not drifting away to the past or jumping ahead to what's going to happen tomorrow. Acceptance is an important part of being mindful, and it's important to understand that from the very beginning. Acceptance means that you're in the moment and accepting it for what it is. You're curious about what's going on and are totally aware of it, although it doesn't mean you have to agree with everything that's happening around you.

Sometimes people get the wrong idea about acceptance. When you accept something, you may not always be okay with what's happening. The first step is to acknowledge or own up to your experience as you're going through it and don't fight it, no matter what it is. In simple terms, you're not acknowledging an experience just to get rid of it or to get it over with. You're acknowledging it without trying to change what it is. After you acknowledge your experience, the next step is to accept it.

Acceptance is useful in everything you do because it helps you change your attitude about things and can lead you to look at whatever you experience, good or bad, in a different and helpful way. Here's an example of how you would bring acceptance to an experience you'd probably consider negative. If you're taking a major test in a subject that gives you shivers or if you're getting a tooth filled, you may want to get it over with quickly. But even then, if you're rooted in the present and go with the experience, it may prove more painless than you thought.

You may think giving your attention to something you don't like would make the experience more unpleasant, but it's often just the opposite. If you pay attention to what's going on and experience it as you're going through it, you can often deal with it more effectively. That's what Mindfulness is all about: staying with the experience, whatever it is, and accepting it for what it is, nothing more, nothing less.

Of course, when you're doing something you find unpleasant like taking a test or when someone says something to you that you don't like, it's not always easy to deal with it. Try staying with it even when you're not thrilled about what's happening. Be aware of the moment without judging it and reacting to it. Try responding instead of reacting. When you react, you act quickly and often without thinking. When you respond, you use your head rather than your emotions.

You may not always be okay with what's going on, but if you tolerate the discomfort and go with it, you'll find it will help in the long run. Have you ever found that thinking about the experience ahead of time can be worse than the experience itself?

Being curious is another way of thinking that will help you practice Mindfulness. It will make acceptance of what's going on in the moment go more smoothly because it will help you keep in touch with what's happening at any particular moment in your life. Curiosity is an important part of Mindfulness because it helps you learn new things. In fact, it's the main idea behind learning anything in life and understanding yourself and others.

If you're curious, you ask yourself and other people a lot of questions like "What could I have eaten today that made my stomach ache?" or "Why did I get so upset when my friend said she couldn't meet me after school?" Curiosity is important in Mindfulness because it helps you become aware of what's happening now. It asks you to pay attention to what's going on around you at this moment.

Are you ready to try being mindful with one activity you're doing today?

TRY IT OUT

Savor What You Eat

When you're eating something you like, eat slowly and enjoy every bite. Slow down the experience so you can get the most out of it. Think about how sometimes when you eat (even something you like), it seems like you never tasted it. Maybe you looked forward to eating your favorite dessert. Before you knew it, you gobbled it up, the experience was over, and you didn't taste any of it.

On the other hand, when you eat mindfully, you notice each bite as it goes into your mouth: the feeling and texture of the food on your tongue, the special taste of it, and the act of chewing and swallowing the food. In other words, you're aware of the whole process of eating as you're doing it. It's not mechanical, as it often is for many people.

Try this with a chocolate morsel—dark, sweet, or semi-sweet, whichever you prefer. Put the chocolate on your tongue and let it sit there. Feel its weight and notice its sweetness. Savor the flavor. Think about how it feels. Experience the thick, creamy texture and the sweet chocolate taste. Wait a couple of minutes before biting into it. This is called *mindful eating*.

Rate Your Food Enjoyment

Try mindful eating the next time you eat, and see how much more you enjoy your meal. In your Mindfulness Journal, rate how much you enjoyed the food on a scale of 1–10.

What number would you rate your enjoyment level before you ate your meal mindfully? What would you rate it after eating mindfully? Ask your parent to try eating the same food mindfully, and compare your experiences. Talk about your experiences with mindful eating in a class discussion.

Be in the Moment No Matter What

It's important to be in the moment all the time, even if you're doing something you're not wild about. Try Mindfulness with a task you don't like. When you're doing an ordinary job that you can't wait to finish like cleaning your room, or another chore you don't enjoy, be aware of each part of the job as you do it: for example, putting things away to declutter your space; organizing your things to make it easier to find them; and throwing away any stuff you don't need.

As you work to complete each job, be aware of what you're doing, and think of how it's helping you feel a sense of doing something positive for yourself. You may not be thrilled about cleaning your room, but you're doing it without judgment, without reacting to it. You are acknowledging (owning up to) and accepting each phase of exactly what it takes to give you a clean, comfortable room.

Write a couple of sentences in your Mindfulness Journal about how you felt about being mindful when you cleaned your room or did another chore you dislike. How was it different from the feeling you usually get about doing this chore? Discuss your findings with the class and compare notes.

Brainstorm with Your Group

Brainstorm with your small group and report back to the class about some uncomfortable things you've experienced that you go through regularly. Use Mindfulness to think of what you'll say to yourself the next time something like this happens. How will it help to go with the feeling instead of trying to block it? Write the answer in your Mindfulness Journal.

Examples of Uncomfortable Experiences

• Worrying about getting a bad grade
• Giving a talk in front of the class
• Disagreeing with your parents

Brainstorm with your small group and report back to the class about how Mindfulness can help make your good experiences even better. Here are some examples:

Examples of Good Experiences

• Appreciating something in nature
• Doing something you enjoy with a friend
• Trying a new food

To the student: In this and all the meditations that follow, say the words in italics in your mind (if you're at home, you can say them in your mind or say them aloud).

MINI MEDITATION

Find a quiet spot. Quiet your mind and settle in. Breathe in and out slowly twice. Think of what it feels like to live in the moment. How would living in the moment help you live a happier life? *I am feeling more and more peaceful. I feel what it's like to be here now, to be awake and aware, to live in the present. When thoughts come and go, I stay with them without reacting or judging them, even if they bother me. I let the thoughts flow, whatever they are, and stay with them. I am living fully in the present. The past is gone, and the future is yet to come. I am present in this moment.*

After a few minutes have passed (one to three minutes), gently open your eyes. Your teacher will tell you when the time is up, or if you're meditating on your own, peek at a clock every so often to see when the time is up.

Chapter Two

Stay Grounded in the Present

BE PRESENT

Staying in the present isn't always easy if you're used to thinking about the future or if you're stuck in the past. But it's interesting that you don't have to try hard to ground yourself in the moment. All you have to do is be there, and new and exciting things will begin to happen for you. For example, you'll worry a lot less because you're living right now instead of back in time or sometime in the future. Have you ever noticed that most of our worries take place when we think too much about the past or the future?

You've seen in the last chapter that an important part of being in the present is acceptance, which means seeing things as they are in the moment. That doesn't mean you have to like what's going on or that you shouldn't care about what matters to you. All it means is that you're looking at what's going on in the moment and saying, "Hey, this is what's happening now, and I'm acknowledging and accepting it." In other words, I may not always agree with what's happening, but I'm staying with it without judging it or getting overly upset over it.

Of course, acceptance never means not standing up for what's important to you or not getting involved if you see an injustice like bullying. In fact, it's quite the opposite. Acceptance means being interested in and curious about what's going on in the moment and being aware and awake to it. In a case like bullying, being aware that it's happening and is causing someone pain can motivate you to take action. If you're aware and you're mindful of a situation you don't like seeing, you can try some things to stop a bad situation.

How can you help yourself stay in the present if you're usually thinking about the past or future? For one thing, if you find yourself moving backward or forward in time more than you'd like to, you can use a word like *present* or a phrase (group of words) like *I am present* to bring yourself back to the moment that is now. Say it aloud or to yourself if others are around.

You can call this your "magic word" because saying it brings you to the present every time you think of it. If you'd prefer, you can make up your own word or nonsense word (for example, *shazam*) to guide you back. Simply say or think your magic word or phrase to return your mind to the present moment.

Try spending some time each day bringing yourself back into the present when you fast forward to the present or rewind to the past. Observe without judging how it makes all your experiences better.

TRY IT OUT

Catch Yourself in the Past or Future

For one day, make a conscious effort to stay grounded in the present. Check how many times you find yourself thinking in the past or future. Make a chart, and mark down how many times you realize you're in different time zones. Then, in the space below the chart, write a short summary of your findings and your reaction to what you discovered. Above all, note how you felt when you were in the present. Is it different from the way you'd usually feel in the same situation?

Ask a parent or another family member to do the activity with you, and then discuss what you both learned about whether you live mainly in the past, present or future. Be prepared to discuss your results with your small group and the entire class.

Instructions

Under each section, draw a small vertical line that shows whether you were thinking in the past, present, or future. You can see where you are for three or more times in one day.

Example: Mindfulness Chart

Past   **Present**   **Future**

In your Mindfulness Journal, write a couple of sentences about whether you are in the past, present, or future on this day. How do you feel about what you discovered?

Also, write a short summary of your findings that you learned from this Mindfulness chart. After everyone has completed the activity, talk about your findings in a small group discussion. Report back to the class what your group members learned by doing the experiment.

Try Staying Grounded in the Present

After you do the previous activity with a parent, ask a classmate to try staying in the present for a day, and then discuss both of your experiences with it. Did it make either or both of you feel different than you usually do? Would you be willing to try being present in the moment for a longer period of time to see if you'd like to make it a part of your life?

Accept Rather Than React

The next time you're tempted to become stressed out about something going on around you, see if you can accept what's happening rather than react to it. Compare your feelings when you respond calmly to a person or event rather than react like you're upset. Write your brief comparison in your Mindfulness Journal. Discuss your experience with acceptance in your small group. A group spokesperson will report back to the class about your group discussion.

Choose Your Own Magic Word

Think of a word or phrase you can use if you want to return to the present rather than living too much in the past or future. In your Mindfulness Journal, write three choices and put a star next to the one you like best. If you want, use one of the ones suggested in this chapter.

MINI MEDITATION

Take a couple of slow, deep breaths until you feel perfectly peaceful and in the moment. Think about what it means to stay grounded in the present rather than the past or future. *I am grounded in the moment. I accept what is happening now, even though I may not always agree with it. I look at what's happening and say, "I am present in this moment." When I begin to think about the past or future, I gently bring myself back to the moment. The moment is what matters most, and I am aware of what is happening in it. I am living fully in the moment. I now claim this moment for myself.*

Chapter Three

Be Patient with Yourself and Others

BE PRESENT

Like most kids, you probably get impatient with other people, especially adults. Did you ever think of how often you get impatient with yourself? One way of getting impatient with yourself is by comparing yourself to other kids when it comes to school, sports, appearance, or friendships. When you think about it, each person has her own talents and abilities, just as you have yours.

If you accept yourself as you are, you'll appreciate yourself more and become more self-confident. Once you stop comparing yourself to other kids, you'll not only see yourself in a more positive light but also see other kids for who they are, rather than as rivals to compete with or top in some way.

We all know that when things are going our way, it's easy to be patient. When you're upset about something, it's much harder because your mind starts racing, and you become stressed. Here's where Mindfulness comes in. It can help you quiet your mind so you can think clearly about what's making you impatient.

The first thing you can do when you feel impatient with a parent, brother or sister, or someone else in your life is stop for a few seconds and recognize the feeling. Tune in and stay with the feeling, and that will help you identify exactly what's upsetting you and how you feel about it. Be curious about it. Ask yourself how it makes you feel physically and mentally to be impatient with this person. Does your body feel tight? Do you feel your palms sweating? Do you feel like shouting or talking back to the person?

If so, try taking a couple of slow, deep breaths. Instead of giving in to impatience and letting it have power over you, stop and think for a moment before saying anything you might feel bad about later.

Here's the bottom line: If you get impatient with yourself or someone else, try using Mindfulness to help you deal with things in a peaceful way. Be curious about how you're feeling, acknowledge how you're feeling, and accept your feeling of impatience. Then you can start dealing with it in a positive way.

TRY IT OUT

List Words That Describe Impatience with Yourself

In your Mindfulness Journal, list three adjectives that tell how you feel when you're impatient with yourself. The next time you're tempted to become impatient with yourself, be curious about the feeling. Why are you feeling this way? What kinds of feelings are you experiencing?

Try not to run away from the feelings that impatience brings you. Acknowledge the feeling of impatience, and stay with it until your thoughts slow down. Afterward, spend a moment thinking about the good things you've done and how you shine in a special way. Discuss with a classmate one of your experiences being impatient with yourself, and listen as he shares one of his experiences with you.

List Ways Impatience Affects Your Body

In your Mindfulness Journal, list three or more things you notice happening in your body when you begin to feel impatient. Write a couple of sentences about how using Mindfulness helps you recognize these feelings and steers you on a better path. Discuss with the entire class and share ideas.

Use Self-Talk to Help Impatience

Self-talk is a way of thinking about how you can solve a problem in a helpful way. All you have to do is talk to yourself in your mind just as you'd talk to someone else who was having the same problem. Take the time to listen to yourself as you would to a friend.

As soon as you start to feel the physical and emotional symptoms that go along with impatience, such as tightness in your muscles and a faster heart rate, take a slow, deep breath. Tune in to the feeling and stay with it. Don't try to brush it off.

Example of Self-Talk to Use When You're Impatient

My heart is starting to race and my muscles feel tight. I don't like the way I feel, but if I go with the feeling and recognize it without judging it, I'll be on the right path.

In your Mindfulness Journal, write a brief script for using self-talk to help your impatience with yourself or others. Use a situation you've actually experienced, or create self-talk based on one of the examples below. Volunteers will share their self-talk scripts with the class.

Sample Situations That May Make You Impatient

- You saw something at the mall you'd love to have. You want to spend your money to buy it, but your parents tell you to wait for your birthday that is six months away.
- Your friend keeps you waiting before a concert you've looked forward to for months. Because of her lateness, you risk missing the first part of the concert.
- You can't seem to score in your favorite sport no matter how hard you try.

Role-Play a Scene

Most people think patience is a virtue, a positive quality that people should work to gain in their lives. With your group, role-play a short scene that shows you behaving impatiently with a family member, such as a parent, brother, or sister. Role-play how you might deal with the problem if you used Mindfulness to help you show patience. Think about a situation that happened to you or a friend, or use one of the following situations.

Sample Situations

- Your neighbor gives you some delicious homemade fudge, and your brother tries to take most of it for himself.
- Your dad tells you if you don't do better on your next report card, you'll be grounded until your grades improve.
- Your mom says you can't go out on school nights, and your best friend is allowed to go out any night she wants.

MINI MEDITATION

Take two slow, deep breaths and relax your body one muscle at a time, moving gradually from your head to your toes. Think about a time when you felt impatient with yourself or others. Imagine how Mindfulness can help you if something similar happens again. *I remember how I feel in my mind and body when I'm patient with myself and other people. I focus on the peacefulness I feel that is the opposite of the stress I feel when impatience strikes. When I feel impatient, I stay with the feeling and am curious about it. I ask myself how it is affecting my mind and body. I acknowledge that I am feeling impatient and accept it. Once I have, I can begin to think more clearly about how to handle impatience in a positive way. Being mindful is a good way to help myself when I become impatient with myself or others.*

Chapter Four

Cut Down on Stress

BE PRESENT

These days, kids face more pressures than ever before. You're pushed to get good grades, take tests and more tests, face doing tons of homework when you get home, and then start all over again the next day.

On top of that, there's the push to look good, fit in with other kids, and excel in activities like sports. Sometimes you wonder when you'll ever have time to relax and do your favorite things, or simply spend some time outside breathing in the calm, clear air. Of course, some stress, like competing in sports or striving for top grades, can keep you moving and motivated, but when stress builds up, you may start to feel its effects on your physical and emotional health.

Mindfulness can definitely help you with the stress you meet every day, whether it comes from school pressures, family disagreements, technology, or even boredom. Be curious about it, like you'd be about a new discovery you've made for a science project you're working on or about a book you've read that explores the possibility of life on other planets.

When you start to feel stress creep up on you, stop for a few seconds and ask yourself questions like these: How am I feeling now? How is stress affecting my body? You may say you're feeling queasy and your hands are clammy or you're breathing harder than you usually do. If you ask how it is affecting your mind, you may say you're feeling tense or angry.

Try not to get caught up in how upset you are and get carried away with the feeling. Simply ask yourself how you're feeling, and describe it to yourself in your mind. Imagine you're looking at what's happening as you would with someone other than yourself. Act like you're an observer rather than a participant in what's happening. When you do this, you'll find the stress

15

you're feeling won't seem as heavy, and you can start to deal with it. Acknowledge the stress and accept it for what it is. Don't fight the feeling. Instead, go with it until it passes.

Once you get in the habit of monitoring your stress levels by noticing how you react with your mind and body, you will be in charge and will find ways to begin to control how deeply you feel stress and how strongly it affects you. Mindfulness is the key. Of course, if you feel that stress is getting to you to the extent it interferes with your ability to be happy or enjoy life, talk to a family member or your school counselor, who will do their best to help you find an answer.

TRY IT OUT

Keep Track of Your Stress Levels

For three days, keep track of when you feel your stress levels building. Try using the Mindfulness technique of looking at what's happening as an observer rather than as a participant. Be interested and inquisitive about it. Ask yourself questions like, "How does the stress make me feel in this moment? What can I do about it?"

In your Mindfulness Journal, make a chart like the one below with the three questions listed. Fill it in for three days. Write about what you learned from making the chart. See how it helps you deal with stress in the future.

Observer Chart

What is causing me to feel stressful?
Day 1:
Day 2:
Day 3:
How does the stress make me feel?
Day 1:
Day 2:
Day 3:
What can I do about it?
Day 1:
Day 2:
Day 3:

Discuss with your group how keeping track of your stress levels helped you deal with stress in your life. Report back to the entire class.

Use Self-Talk If You Feel Stress before Something Happens

Have you ever tried out for a sports team or a school show? For some kids, anticipating something stressful is the hardest part. They feel more nervous and uncertain as the day draws near. They're thinking, "Will I make it?" instead of being in the moment and going with the feelings that may sometimes make them uncomfortable. Can you think of something you've experienced, like going to the dentist, that didn't seem as bad after it happened?

Think about how anticipating something ahead of time can give you more stress. Picture yourself trying out for a team or a school show. Before the big day, you may have asked yourself, "What will it be like when I'm actually trying out? Will I get through it okay?"

You may have found that when you tried out, you somehow overcame your nervousness and gave it your best. When you tried out, you got caught up in the moment, not giving much thought to whether or not you'd make the team or get the part in the play. You may have actually enjoyed the process because you went with the flow and threw yourself into what you were doing rather than worrying about the end result. You accepted the moment for what it was.

When you go with and stay with the experience rather than trying to block it, you're more likely to find yourself in control of the situation and end up feeling confident and powerful.

When you stay with the experience, be curious. Ask yourself how you're feeling in your body and mind. Do you have physical symptoms like a racing heart or symptoms in your mind like nervous thoughts?

What can you say to yourself if you feel that stress may hurt your performance? Remember that it's okay to feel some stress before you try out for something. But it's also important for you to stay in control and not let stress take over. Think about what you learned in the last section about self-talk.

In your Mindfulness Journal, write one or two sentences you'll say to yourself to help you when you try out for an activity. Hint: Don't try to fight the nervousness. Feel it, stay with it, and then move on. Volunteers will read their self-talk sentences to the class.

Share your ideas with the class about how Mindfulness can help you deal with stressful situations you've dealt with, such as impatience, taking a test, or trying out for a sport, the school show, or other school activity.

Boredom Can Be a Form of Stress

Many kids feel bored sometime during the course of a day. You may feel it when sitting in a class that doesn't excite you or when you can't seem to motivate yourself to get up and go.

Have you ever thought that boredom can also be a type of stress? Boredom is actually the opposite of Mindfulness because it means you're waiting for something to come into your life. As you know, Mindfulness is being content and feeling fine in the present moment. Think of it this way: If you're fully aware of the present moment, it's pretty hard to feel bored.

Mindfulness can help by giving you a way to deal with boredom. Instead of fighting your feelings of boredom and feeling stressed about it, be with it and see what comes from the feeling. Sometimes boredom can give you the chance to become more creative. Surprise yourself. See what exciting ideas you can dream up in the midst of a bout with boredom.

The next time you're bored, go with the feeling and don't judge it. Instead, be curious about it. Ask yourself: *What does being bored feel like? Why am I bored in this moment? How do I feel about it? What can I do about it?* Once you acknowledge the feeling of boredom for what it is and accept it, you can begin to do something about it. Stay with the boredom and see where it leads you. Maybe it will turn out to be a springboard for a new hobby or interest.

Try Mindful Walking to Banish Boredom

If you're sitting around the house feeling bored, you may want to try mindful walking to soften your feeling of boredom and spark your creativity. Your walk will energize you to begin accepting your feeling of boredom and help propel you into an action mode.

Mindful walking is a form of meditation that helps you connect with yourself and your surroundings. Start your walk and think about how the ground feels under your feet. Feel the lightness or heaviness of each step. Hear the crunch of the leaves, the softness of the damp ground, or the hardness of the concrete.

Be fully conscious of the experience of walking around your neighborhood or in nature (the park or the beach, for example). When you complete your walk, acknowledge the feeling of boredom you've been experiencing and accept it. Instead of giving in to boredom, try using your feelings of boredom as a tool for jumpstarting your creative mind.

Discuss How Boredom Can Help You Be More Creative

Brainstorm with the entire class how you think boredom might lead you to try some new adventures. How can Mindfulness help when you're bored? The teacher or a class recorder writes ideas on the board. Try one you like the next time you're bored.

MINI MEDITATION

Start by taking two slow, deep breaths. Relax your entire body one step at a time. What would it be like if you could lessen stress in your life? What effects would it have on your mind and body? *I am coping with any stress that comes my way. By putting myself in the moment and thinking about how my body feels, I am becoming aware of how stress affects me. Instead of running away from stress, I accept it as a part of life and deal with it as it comes. When I feel stressful, I can deal with it better by taking a moment to stay with the feeling, even if it's not pleasant. I can be curious about it and ask myself how I'm feeling. Self-talk can also help me cope with stress. Once I accept the feelings stress brings me, I can start to move past the uncomfortable feelings that go along with it.*

Chapter Five

Using Technology Mindfully

BE PRESENT

Technology brings great advances to your life with the Internet, video games, and Smartphones, but it also has a downside. You stay connected, but at the same time, you can get so caught up in technology that you're living in a virtual world, sometimes out of touch with the people around you.

Did you ever get the feeling that even though you're sitting with a friend or family member, you're actually a million miles away when you're texting or playing video games? It's hard to be in the moment when technology takes over your brain and makes it difficult to tune in to what others are saying.

You may not think using technology could become a problem because it's so much a part of your life, but if you think about it, it can sometimes invade your sense of living in the moment. Of course, we all know that being connected by technology has its good points. Information's always at your fingertips, you can be in touch with people instantly, and you can enjoy playing games by yourself or with friends.

Mindfulness will help you use technology wisely. If you're mindful when you use technology, you'll think about when it's wise to use it and when it's better to tune it out.

Of course it's best to tune out when you're talking with your family and friends or doing homework, unless you're using technology for an assignment.

When you're around your family and friends and you're also tuned in to technology, stop for a moment and ask yourself if you'd like to continue using your electronic device or if you could hold off until you're finished talking and listening.

Here are some questions you could ask if you wanted to be curious about how you're using technology: *Can I listen to my friend and tune in to my Smartphone or tablet at the same time? What would happen if I waited to use my electronic devices and decided to take the time to talk with my family without electronic distractions? How would I feel about giving my full attention to my friend or family member instead of tuning in to technology while we're talking?*

TRY IT OUT

Keep Track of How Much Time You Use Technology

For two days on a weekend, keep a record of how much time you spend using technology.

This chart will help you list all the forms of technology you use morning, afternoon, and night. Use the abbreviations below to show what kinds of technology you use. Write approximately how much time you spend during each time period using them.

Abbreviations: Smartphone (SP), computer (C), tablet (T)

If you use other forms of technology, list them and use your own abbreviations.

Sample Technology Chart with Abbreviations and Times

Morning	Afternoon	Night
SP 20 minutes	C 1 hour	T 2 hours

After you gather your research about the time you spent using technology over a two-day period and talk about it in your small group, discuss the following questions and report back to the class:

- How much time each day (outside of schoolwork) do you think is a fair amount to spend on technology?
- How does it compare with the time you spend?
- What are the positive and negative points about each form of technology you use every day?

How Does Technology Affect Your Relationships?

For two days, stop and be mindful of every time you use technology while communicating with your family and friends. Compare how it felt with the time you spent mindfully listening and talking with them.

In your Mindfulness Journal, write a few sentences describing how it felt when you gave your full attention to family and friends versus when you used technology when you talked with them. Use these questions to help you write your answers:

- What can happen when I use technology like texting, e-mailing, or playing video games when I'm communicating with my family and friends?
- How does it make me feel when my family and friends use technology when we're spending time together?
- Is it possible to be tuned into technology and, at the same time, give my attention to the people around me?

Talk about these questions in your small group, and then compare notes in a class discussion.

How Does Using Technology Wisely Help You Communicate Better

Write a skit (short play) with your small group that shows two people trying to communicate while using technology (e.g., parent and child, two friends, or grandparent and grandchild). Write a companion skit that shows the same people communicating without using technology.

Divide your group so that a few students write the first skit and other students in the group write the second.

Perform your skits for the class, and stage a class discussion about how the conversations in the two skits were different.

MINI MEDITATION

Take two deep relaxing breaths and, at your own pace, get into your meditation mode. No hurry, no worry. Think about how you use technology and whether you are satisfied with it or want to make a change. *I am using technology mindfully. I know when technology will help me learn, enjoy time with friends, and connect with people near and far. I also know there are times when it's better to connect with people rather than devices, when it's time to talk and listen without the time and energy using technology involves.*

I put technology in perspective by making it one part of my day rather than the most important part of my day. When I use technology in a mindful way, I enjoy my relationships more because I am there for the people I'm with as I want them to be there for me.

Chapter Six

Talk to Get Results

BE PRESENT

Mindfulness can help you in a big way with your communication skills. You know how important it is for people to hear what you're saying and understand your message. Yet sometimes you may feel frustrated when you're talking to parents, teachers, and friends. You try your best to express your feelings about something really important to you, but probably, more than you'd like to admit, your attempts end up in anger, frustration, or both.

But no worries, Mindfulness can help you talk with your family and friends so you get your message across in a way that makes the people you're with hear and understand what you're saying.

The road to mindful speaking involves some simple principles, but like all the other aspects of Mindfulness, you have to be willing to practice until you feel comfortable using them. To begin, let's review three types of ways people communicate with others. Which way of talking and listening most applies to you? Read the descriptions below to find out.

Passive Communicator

Some people communicate in a passive way. That's what you would do if your main goal were for other people to like you. But there's a downside to being passive when you talk with people. It can often make you feel unhappy with yourself because you're not saying how you really feel.

You may feel angry later that you hid behind your words and didn't say exactly how you felt. When you talk to people in a passive way, you feel like you're not getting your point across, and it can upset you to think they're not hearing you.

People who tend to apologize a lot when they haven't really done anything wrong are passive communicators.

Examples of Passive Communication

- A classmate asks to see your report for history that you've spent a long time writing. She doesn't feel like doing all the work herself. You say, "Sure, no problem." However, you feel angry afterward because you didn't want to give it to her after all the work you did, but you also didn't want to take the chance of losing her as a friend.
- Your parent says you're not working hard enough when you get a poor grade in math. You say, "Sorry. I wish I could do better. I guess I don't take after you because I don't understand math no matter how hard I try. I don't know why math is such a problem for me."

Aggressive Communicator

Some people communicate in an aggressive way. If you always feel you have to be right and sometimes drown out the other person by talking forcefully, you may be an aggressive communicator.

Examples of Aggressive Communication

- Your mom tells you to start your homework right away. You say, "Stop bugging me. You're always on me to do something. I never get any free time."
- Your little sister asks you to play a game with her. You say, "Can't you see I'm busy talking to my friend? I don't have time now."

People who communicate this way like to boss people around and want to feel like they're always in charge. If you use very strong words and yell to get your point across, you're probably an aggressive communicator.

Often aggressive people feel sorry about how they treated someone after they speak to someone that way. Because of the way they speak, aggressive communicators have the most trouble getting along with parents and teachers. They also have a hard time making and keeping friends because of their "in-your-face" way of talking.

Assertive Communicators

On the other hand, there are some people who know how to communicate in a totally different way. They're called assertive communicators, and they may hold the secret to a powerful way of speaking so that others listen to their ideas even if they disagree.

Assertiveness helps us talk in a way that makes people pay attention to what we're saying. Being assertive also benefits us because it helps us feel confident and strong. It helps us show respect to others, and it helps other people respect us.

Examples of Assertive Communication

- A friend hurts your feelings by saying something unkind about you to another friend behind your back. You say, "I didn't like hearing what you said about me. We need to talk about it."
- Your brother says you're not doing your best when you play baseball with your team. You say, "I feel really bad when you say that. I'd like it if you tried to help me stay positive about my game. It might help me do better."

To be an assertive communicator, you need to state your thoughts clearly, honestly, and respectfully and to give the people you're talking with the chance to express their feelings. Assertive communicators are usually laid-back and sometimes sprinkle what they say with humor. They choose their words carefully and never say things that hurt others. Most importantly, they treat others fairly.

TRY IT OUT

Discover Your Main Form of Communication

How can you use what you've learned about Mindfulness to help you become more aware of the way you communicate with people, both kids and adults? You can start by being curious. Ask the person you're talking with questions to better understand his point of view. Being curious by asking these questions also helps you acknowledge what the person is saying even if you don't accept everything you're hearing.

If you get upset when you're talking with someone, use self-talk to help you describe how you're feeling. Inspire yourself by giving yourself some encouragement at the end of your self-talk. You'll find that using the Mindfulness techniques you've learned will help your conversations run much more smoothly.

Answer These Questions in Your Mindfulness Journal

- How do *you* talk to people? What is your main form of communication: aggressive, passive, or assertive?
- If the type of communication you're using isn't working for you, which type of communication would you like to try?

Volunteers will share their answers in a class discussion.

Write Dialogues for Three Ways of Talking

With your small group, write a short dialogue for each method of communication: passive, aggressive, and assertive, listed in the "Be Present" section above. Students in the group show how they would talk to a friend or parent about an issue that's bothering them. See the examples below for topic ideas.

For the first dialogue, a student is a passive communicator, for the second, another student acts like an aggressive communicator, and for the third, another student takes on the role of an assertive communicator. Use the same situation for each conversation.

Here are a few ideas for situations your group can write about, or the group can make up its own.

- Your parent tells you you're not allowed to go out until you finish cleaning your room.
- Your teacher accuses you of misbehaving, and it wasn't your fault.
- Someone does not get back to his friend about plans for the weekend.

Pattern your scripts after the examples below that use one of your own situations or the situations listed above. Here are examples of scripts using the three forms of communication. In the examples below, a student in the group, the one playing the "you" part, is the communicator trying different ways of talking to someone.

After writing scripts about the three different ways of communicating, act them out for the class and discuss them.

Situation: Someone does not get back to his friend about plans for the weekend.

Examples of Dialogues Using the Three Forms of Communication

Passive Communicator

Friend: What's wrong?

You (looking down): Nothing. What makes you think anything's wrong?

Friend: You're being very quiet, and I think you're angry with me.

You: I don't want to talk about it.

Aggressive Communicator

You: Some friend *you* are, not getting back to me about what we're doing this weekend! You can never make up your mind.

Friend: Sometimes I don't get around to making plans until the last minute. I don't see what the problem is.

You (walking away): Well, you can just forget it now. I've already made other plans.

Assertive Communicator

You: I need to know if we're doing anything this weekend so I can make plans. Let me know your ideas.

Friend: I'm really sorry I didn't let you know. Something came up, and I haven't had time to think about it yet. I'll let you know tonight, okay?

You: That's fair. We'll talk about it then.

Write About How Talking with Different Types of Speakers Makes You Feel

When I talk with each type of communicator: passive, aggressive, or assertive, how does it make me feel? In your Mindfulness Journal, write two adjectives describing how you feel when you talk with each type of communicator. Discuss and compare your ideas with the class's ideas.

Create Cartoons about Different Speaking Styles

Work with a partner: Create a cartoon using stick figures or drawings. Use poster board, and make the figures and words large so you can show your cartoons to the class.

Write captions for each of the three speaking styles: passive, aggressive, and assertive. Don't label the speaking styles. For each style, use two captions, one person talking about something that bothers her, and the other replying in each of the three speaking styles. Use the same situation for each drawing. Exchange drawings with another student, and see if both of you can correctly identify the speaking styles that the other student has drawn.

Volunteers share their cartoons with the class and see if the class can figure out the communication styles used.

Role-Play a Scene Showing Assertive Communication

Work with a partner: Use one of the situations below, or make up your own. Show how you can talk in an assertive way when you're upset about something. Think about the Mindfulness tips you've studied: Stay grounded in the present moment. Use your magic word to take you there. Be curious. Acknowledge and accept the situation even if you don't totally agree with it. Use self-talk to calm yourself before you talk to the other person. Then play it out in your mind before you begin to speak. Your teacher will choose volunteers to present your dialogues to the class.

Sample Situations

• You're upset about a poor grade you got in gym. Talk to your gym teacher about it.
• Your brother calls you names and hurts your feelings.
• Your classmate says you made the basketball team lose the game.

MINI MEDITATION

Take two slow, deep breaths and calm your body, starting with your head and slowly moving down to your feet. Take your time, and get into your peaceful mode at your own pace. Think about these questions: How do I communicate with my friends and family? Am I expressing my feelings and opinions in an open, honest way? *I talk to others as I would want them to talk to me, with kindness and respect. I do my best to think about stating my thoughts clearly, and with concern for the person I'm talking to always in the back of my mind. I can agree or disagree with someone, but when I talk mindfully, I'm always tuned into the moment.*

Chapter Seven

Listen Up!

BE PRESENT

How you listen when others are talking is just as important as how you talk to them. Mindfulness can help you be a good listener because when you're truly focusing on the present, you'll want to hear what people say and show them you care about them by giving them your full attention.

Sometimes it isn't easy to listen when someone is criticizing you or giving a completely different opinion from yours. It's hard to hear what they're saying without wanting to interrupt and give your own opinion, but it pays to listen before responding. Take a moment to tune in, and let your friend or family member say what's on his mind. Then respond, using mindful, assertive language.

How do you use Mindfulness to listen? First of all, you stay grounded in the present and act as if no one else is around except for the person you're talking with. Be curious about what the person is saying. Ask questions to show you're interested. Give the person your full attention before stating your opinion. It's tempting to interrupt, but waiting to hear what someone has to say often pays off. If you listen, she'll be more likely to listen to you. Most of the time, if you listen respectfully, the person you're talking to will grant you the same courtesy. Acknowledge what he's saying and accept it even if you don't agree.

Eye contact shows people you're interested in what they have to say. However, this doesn't mean staring them down or making them feel uncomfortable. Simply be there, as you'd like them to be there for you when you have something important to communicate. It goes without saying that you'll want to turn off electronic devices and the TV and tune out any other distractions. Make what your friend or family member is saying the only thing that matters.

Mindful listening also includes the listening we do every day, such as listening to music. Think about how the music comes together with the words to give listeners a message. Do you like the message the music gives? Did you discover anything different when you listened mindfully to the music you usually play, versus the time you didn't pay close attention to it?

Try mindful listening the next time someone disagrees or criticizes you, or when someone simply wants to talk. Also use it to tune in better to all the sounds around you, including music.

TRY IT OUT

Role-Play Mindful Listening

With a partner, role-play a situation in which you and a friend disagree about something. Create your own role-play, or use one of the situations below. Show how you can listen mindfully to your friend. Demonstrate how you would speak mindfully after you listen to your friend. Be curious about how she feels. Ask your friend questions to help you understand her feelings better. Try not to get angry or judge what she's saying. Just listen and then respond.

After you role-play mindful listening with a partner, the teacher will ask volunteers to present their role-plays to the class.

Sample Role-Play Situations

- You and your friend disagree on where to go this weekend.
- Your friend dislikes one of your other friends and doesn't want to hang out with you when the other friend is around.
- Your classmate gets angry about something you said.

Listen Mindfully to Connect with an Older Relative

When older relatives such as grandparents visit, spend some time listening to what they're saying without any electronic distractions. Be curious about them and their lives. Ask questions. Make up your own, or use the ones below. Acknowledge what they're saying, and look interested by using positive body language and talk. Think about staying around and talking for a while without rushing off to your room. Did you find the time you spent with them more rewarding when you took the time to listen and respond mindfully? Make a mental note of it. In your Mindfulness Journal write briefly about how the conversation went. Share your experience in a class discussion.

Sample Questions to Ask an Older Relative

- What things did you like to do when you were my age?
- What did you like best about growing up when you did?
- How was life different for you than it is for kids growing up now?
- What is your best advice for kids my age?

Listen and Then Speak Mindfully

With a partner, role-play one of the following scenes, or make up your own, in which someone criticizes you. Use mindful listening, and speak in an assertive but kind way. Take a moment to tune in. Be curious by asking questions about why the person feels this way. Acknowledge and accept what he says. Listen, and try not to interrupt, even though you may be tempted to, until the person finishes.

- Your parent criticizes the clothes you chose to wear to school.
- Your classmate says you're a show-off.
- Your friend accuses you of being the teacher's pet.

Present your role-plays to the class.

Listen to Music Mindfully

If you listen to your favorite music, try listening in a mindful way. What message is the singer trying to convey with the words and music in the song? Instead of seeing the song only as background music while you're doing other things, listen as you never have before. Write a sentence in your Mindfulness Journal about what you think the main message of the music is.

How did you feel when you listened to the song in a mindful way compared to when you listened to it without using Mindfulness?

Volunteers will discuss their findings with the class.

MINI MEDITATION

Take a couple of slow, deep breaths. Let the air fill your lungs, and bring your awareness to the present moment. Imagine what it would be like if you could truly listen to what your friends and family say instead of rushing to get your point across.

When I listen to others, it gives me a true understanding of where they're coming from and offers a new appreciation of who they are. When I truly listen, I'll find my life is more peaceful. Conflicts and arguments won't happen as much and will disappear more quickly. I'll try listening and responding kindly to everyone I meet today. I'm tuning in, being curious, acknowledging, and accepting. I am present now for others, listening to others as I want them to listen to me.

Chapter Eight

Be Positive When You Speak

BE PRESENT

It's tempting when we're upset with someone to speak in a negative way. For example, when your mom says you can't meet your friends at the pizza place, you might say to her: "You never let me do anything, so you probably won't let me meet my friends at Perfect Pizza at the mall. All the other kids can go, and it makes me feel like I'm in grade school when you don't let me do things my friends are allowed to do."

Instead, you may want to frame your request more positively. Here's an example: "I'm hoping you'll let me go to the pizza place at the mall with my friends. I know some parents think kids can get in trouble hanging out there, but I promise I'll keep safe by staying with friends and won't get in trouble."

Wait for your parent to respond. If the answer is *no*, say this: "Can you think about it? You know I'm pretty responsible. We could try it and see how it goes."

If your parent agrees, your positive speaking skills have paid off. There will be times, of course, when your parents will say *no* to your request, and it will be important for you to trust their decision. It may not always be easy, but sometimes acceptance is the best way to go. One of the things Mindfulness teaches is that acceptance can be a good thing even though we may not always feel that way.

Listen in on this conversation between Jay and Todd, two friends, to show how positive communication can make a difference.

Jay: You said you'd go to the movies with me this weekend, and now you're backing out.

35

Todd: I just found out my cousin is coming from California, and I don't get to see him often. We'll go next week.

Jay: Some friend you are. I'll get someone else to go.

Todd: What brought that on?

Fast forward to a different scene with Jay communicating in a more positive way.

Jay: I wish you'd think about going to the movies with me this weekend like we'd planned. I know your cousin's coming in from California, and you haven't seen him in a while. I'm wondering if you could ask him to go with us to the movie. We've been waiting to see it a long time. And besides, after all the great stuff you've told me about your cousin, I'd like to meet him.

Todd: I like that idea. Why didn't I think of it? Okay, I'll text my cousin and let him know. You two will get along great.

As you can see, when you use words in a positive way, people are more likely to consider your ideas. You may not always get what you want, but the adults and kids in your life will appreciate your mature attitude and your willingness to understand where they're coming from.

Another way you can use positive speech, a mindful way of talking, is to express your dissatisfaction with what someone is doing in a gentler way than you usually might. For example, instead of saying to your parent, "You yell at me for everything. I'm sick of it," you could say something like: "It hurts when you yell at me all the time, and it hurts even more when I yell back. I wish we could get along better. Can we talk about it?"

Try using key phrases like "Can we talk about it?"; "I'm hoping we can find a middle ground"; or "Let's see if we can get together on this."

You can use positive talk with anybody you talk to every day: parents, friends, brothers, sisters, and even teachers. The main thing is to take the high road and use positive talk to get your point across. It's one more way of being mindful.

TRY IT OUT

Think of Four Positive Sentences

Think about how framing your request more positively can help you communicate better. In your Mindfulness Journal, write four sentences you can use to help you talk positively and get better results. Talk about your ideas in a class discussion. The class can brainstorm more ideas for positive sentences as the teacher writes them on the board.

Example: "I'm hoping we can find an answer."

Try using a sentence like this the next time you're having a difficult conversation. On a day the teacher assigns, report back to the class about how it worked for you.

Role-Play a Time You Got Upset with Your Parents

Think of a time you were upset with your parents. With a classmate, role-play a situation, or one below, to show how you'd use positive speech to work out the problem. In some cases, try making the situation end positively even when you don't get what you want.

- Your mom and dad won't let you play video games on school nights.
- Your parents won't let you try out for another sports team. (You're in two already.)
- Your mom says skateboards of any kind are dangerous, and you can't spend the money you've saved up to buy one.

Think of Something Better to Say to Your Parent When You're Angry

In your Mindfulness Journal, write something negative that kids sometimes say to their parents that often makes things worse. Then write a better (more positive) way of saying the same thing. Discuss with the class.

Examples

Negative Way: "I hate you."
Better Way: "I feel sad and upset when you yell at me."
Negative Way: "I don't feel like cleaning my room now. You're always bugging me about something."
Better Way: "I'll do it soon, if that's okay with you. I just need a little break after doing all this homework."

Role-Play a Time You Disagreed with a Friend

With your group, write a script based on a time you disagreed with a friend, or use one of the ideas below. Show how you can be positive with your speech when responding to a friend. Act it out for the class. Afterward, have a class discussion about how the positive speech worked in each situation.

Sample Situations

- You and your friend disagree about what to do on your day off from school.

- You and your friend are partners in a class project. You have different ideas about what will work best.
- You and your friend try out for a sports team. One of you makes it and the other doesn't. One of you feels hurt, and you get into an argument.

MINI MEDITATION

Breathe in and out slowly a couple of times until you feel rested and mellow. Think about how using positive rather than negative words can help you avoid and solve conflicts. *I can find more harmony and less conflict if I stress the positive when I try to resolve a problem. Whenever I find myself getting angry with someone, I take a deep breath and root myself in the moment. I go with the feeling and stay with it without trying to banish it. I stay in the moment without judging the situation or reacting to it. Because I use positive talk, I find it easier to compromise even if I don't totally agree with what someone is saying. I accept whatever happens as it is.*

Chapter Nine

Use *I* Instead of *You*

BE PRESENT

Like everything in Mindfulness, using *I* instead of *you* is simple and effortless. All you have to do is use the word *I* more often than you use the word *you* when you talk to friends and family, and you're on your way. Along with the other techniques in this book, using *I* messages will help you become a more assertive and effective communicator.

When you're in the middle of a hot and heavy conversation, try using *I* messages. When you use *you* instead of *I*, it can sound like you're blaming the other person, and that may make a problem even worse.

- Example of *you* message: "You're always picking on me."
- Example of *I* message: "I feel bad when you say those things to me."

The first step, of course, whenever you're trying to get your point across is to ground yourself in the moment. Take a couple of deep breaths. Tune in and listen to what the other person says, even if you don't agree or like what she's saying. Be curious. Ask questions so you can understand her ideas better. Acknowledge what she says even if you don't agree with it. It may not be what you believe, but it's that person's way of thinking. After you acknowledge and accept what she is saying, use an *I* statement to reply. Here's an example of how you can use *I* messages to respond to people.

Consider this scene: You're helping your dad paint the house and you spill paint on the floor. Your dad gets angry and says, "Why do you have to do everything so fast? Now look at the mess you've made."

You could act angry and intimidated and say, "You're always mean to me. You're not like my friends' dads," and start a big argument, or you could say something like this: "I feel upset when you talk to me like that. Spilling the paint was an accident. I'll start cleaning it up."

This response would be more likely to give your dad an idea of how you feel. The fact that you used an *I* message helped get your point across and also helped you remain calm instead of reacting angrily to what your father said.

This technique is also useful when someone is using words to insult you. Here's an example of a conversation between two classmates, Sara and Carrie.

Carrie: What happened to your hair? Why did you get it chopped off? It looks weird that way.

Sara: I don't like it when people criticize the way I look. It hurts, and I don't appreciate the put-down.

Surprised that Sara doesn't take the bait, Carrie shrugs and walks away.

Of course, if Carrie continues talking to Sara in an unkind way, or if her comments get worse, Sara would want to talk to her parent, counselor, or another adult she trusts about how Carrie is treating her. However, it often helps to use *I* statements to halt unkind remarks before they spiral out of control.

The next time someone says something that hurts your feelings or tries to start an argument, cut it short with *I* messages. This way of talking usually makes people think about what they said and how they said it. Using *I* instead of *you* can go a long way to prevent hurt feelings, keep arguments from getting out of hand, and create more peace in your life. It's one more way to communicate mindfully.

TRY IT OUT

Practice Saying *I* Instead of *You*

Change three *you* statements into *I* statements, and see how it makes a difference. Write the three examples in your Mindfulness Journal. Give the *you* statement first, and write the *I* statement under it. Discuss examples with the entire class.

Example

> *You* statement: "You're never on my side when Bob (my brother) bothers me."
>
> *I* statement: "I feel bad when you think I'm the cause of all our arguments."

Discuss How Using *I* Statements Can Help

Discuss with your small group: Name a situation when using *I* statements could have helped you avoid a disagreement. Exchange stories about how you could have better dealt with a problem using *I* statements. Report back to the class.

Write a Dialogue Using *You* and *I* Statements

Work with a partner. Write a short dialogue using *you* statements. Rewrite the dialogue using *I* statements. Create your own statements or use the examples below. Exchange dialogues with another pair of partners in your class. Each of you will tell the other why you think your *I* statement dialogues will work better than the ones using *you*. Volunteers will share their *you* and *I* statements with the class.

Ideas for Dialogues

- A classmate wants to use your ideas for a class project without giving you credit.
- Your younger brother or sister always borrows your things without asking you first.
- Your parent accuses you of doing something you didn't do.

Brainstorm a List of Times *I* Statements Will Help

With the entire class, brainstorm at least five occasions when using *I* statements can help you. What words would you use in your *I* statements to help you deal with what the person said to you? Try using an *I* statement with a family member or friend, and report back to the class about how it worked for you. See the examples below for ideas.

Examples

- When teasing gets out of hand with a friend, or when your brother or sister calls you a name
- When your parent criticizes you for forgetting to do a chore
- When your teacher says you're not working hard enough but you honestly don't understand the math

MINI MEDITATION

Take two deep breaths, and let a feeling of peacefulness wash over you. Remember the last time someone said something to criticize or hurt you and how it ended. Picture yourself using *I* statements instead of *you* statements to make what happened have a happier ending. *I ask questions to understand someone better. I listen to and acknowledge the other person's feelings even if I don't agree. I use self-talk to help keep myself calm. I speak assertively but softly to the person and will use* I *statements the next time someone says hurtful things to me. No matter what someone says, I can choose how to respond. Saying* I *works better than saying* you.

Chapter Ten

Put Yourself in Another Person's Shoes

BE PRESENT

Another important part of mindful communication is putting yourself in another person's shoes so that you can better understand exactly how he feels. This simply means doing your best to actually put yourself in another person's place in order to understand how he thinks about things.

You may not always agree with how other people feel or think about an issue, but if you put yourself in their place, it will help give you a better idea of how they see things. That may be very different from the way you do. For example, when you're talking with someone like a parent, sibling, or classmate, stop for a moment before responding. Tune in to what he's saying, and stay with it before starting to talk. Resist the temptation to judge or react. Instead, really listen to what he's saying without jumping in and giving your opinion. This way, you'll find it easier to be totally in the moment with the person.

Make eye contact with the person you're with, and hear what she's saying as you've never heard before. Be curious about how the person's feeling. Ask yourself if you think she's feeling happy, sad, excited, or angry. Notice the way she talks and observe her body language. Before you respond, be with the person.

If you don't understand her point, be curious and ask questions about it. For example, you could say, "Do you want to tell me a little more about that?" or "I want to understand what's going on. Asking, "Can we talk about it?" is another way of showing you're doing your best to think and feel as she does. Don't push for answers. Just let her know you're there for her.

Make your body language open rather than closed. Keep your arms relaxed rather than crossed. Nod your head once in a while, showing you understand and accept what she's saying, even if you may not totally agree with her position.

Here's a dialogue in which the speaker puts herself in the place of the person she's talking with by putting herself in the other person's shoes. Devon is talking with her friend Melissa about why Devon's parents won't let her walk around town with her friends after school.

Melissa: Why do you look so upset? What's bothering you?

Devon: I'm the only kid who can't walk around town with my friends after school. You and all the other kids can go to the coffee shop and the other stores, and I have to go straight home from school like a little kid. It's not fair.

Melissa: (Stopping for a minute and trying to put herself in Devon's place) I can see why you're upset. Have you tried talking to your parents again?

Devon: Yes, but they won't listen.

Melissa: I hear you. But when you think about it, you'd have to walk home part of the way alone because you live pretty far from the other kids, and that might not be safe.

Devon: But I'm the only one who can't go places after school. You've heard some of the other kids tease me about it.

Melissa: I know how that must make you feel. I'd say try talking to your parents again. Ask when they'd feel comfortable letting you go with us.

Devon: I know what they'll say. But maybe I'll try anyway. It can't hurt.

Melissa: And if they say *no*, you'll at least have an idea of when they'll consider letting you go into town with us.

Devon: Hey, thanks for listening.

Melissa: No problem. Let me know if you need to talk more.

We don't know if Devon's parents will reconsider and let her go into town after school with her friends. However, because Melissa listened to Devon by putting herself in her friend's place, Devon came out of the conversation feeling better that someone cared enough to understand exactly how she felt. Melissa acted curious about her friend's problems, she acknowledged what Devon said without judging, and she used *I* messages when she talked to her.

When you put yourself in another person's shoes as Melissa did, you're mindful of their feelings and give them the amazing gift of being a mindful listener.

TRY IT OUT

Think of Ways to Help by Truly Listening

Write the answers to the next two questions in your Mindfulness Journal, and then share your ideas with other students in a class discussion.

- List two ways you can put yourself in another person's shoes. How can Mindfulness help you do this? If you've ever put yourself in another's person's shoes, describe how it felt to you. How did it help the person?
- List three adjectives showing how you feel when people truly listen to you by putting themselves in your place.

Use Positive Body Language When You Listen

What kinds of things can you do to show you're listening to what people say when they're talking? In your Mindfulness Journal, write three ways you can show through your body language that you're listening and care about the person. Try using positive body language when you put yourself in another person's shoes. On a day the teacher chooses, report back to the class about how using positive body language helped you put yourself in another person's shoes.

Put Yourself in Another Person's Shoes

With a partner, write a short scene like the one in the "Be Present" section in this chapter. Here's the situation: Your friend has a problem, and you are helping him by putting yourself in his shoes. Act out the scene for the class to show how helpful it is to put yourself in his situation. In a class discussion, give your opinion about how effective the techniques in the skits were.

MINI MEDITATION

Take two or more deep breaths to let out any stress or tension you're feeling. Think of what it would be like if you could listen to friends or family members and actually feel the way they do. *I see things in a new and different way and help those I care about by listening with my ears and with my heart. I can remember a time that someone cared enough to listen when I needed advice or had a problem. I remember how it made all the difference because that person put herself in my shoes instead of seeing things only from her own viewpoint. The next time someone needs me to be truly present, I will try putting myself in the other person's place.*

Chapter Eleven

Get Along Better with Your Family

BE PRESENT

You may want to start practicing your mindful speaking and listening skills with your family. You probably know that kids are more likely to have disagreements with their close relatives than with their friends. It stands to reason this would happen because you're with your family more than you are with anyone else. Emotions can sometimes get out of hand when people are close to one another in a family setting.

Let's review the ways you can use Mindfulness to boost your speaking and listening skills; in this case, with your close relatives. When you talk to your family, consider using assertive communication, giving your message in a brief, straightforward, respectful way without being passive, meaning wishy-washy and not to the point, or aggressive, meaning angry and irritable. Above all, be positive when you talk. It definitely works better than being negative.

It's also important to be a good listener with your relatives because it's easy to tune them out, especially if they tend to repeat the same thing. Sometimes they may feel they have to repeat things because they don't think you're listening. If they think you're listening, they won't have to say it as many times.

When you listen, look at the person talking and try not to interrupt. Be curious about what he's saying. Ask him questions so you can better understand what he's saying. Tune in to what he says even if you may not be thrilled with it. Also, be sure you're not multitasking by using your electronic devices. Nothing will turn off someone talking to you more than having to compete with Smartphones, TVs, computers, or video games. After the person finishes talking, be curious. Ask questions so you can better understand what your family member's saying.

Another important part of mindful talking is using *I* messages instead of *you* messages. When you're conversing with close family members, like parents or siblings, sometimes it's tempting to start blaming them for everything. Using *I* instead of *you* instantly cools things down and softens hard feelings. Finally, it helps a lot to put yourself in another's shoes because it shows you're making an effort to understand this person's point of view.

Now that we've recapped the main ideas behind mindful speaking and listening, let's consider some scenarios where you could practice using these techniques with your family.

Picture this: Your mom asks you to help with chores. She's exhausted from work and often gets angry about you not pitching in around the house. By the time you do your homework, you want a little time to yourself, and that's understandable. Chore wars always seem to end up in an argument, but what if you tried mindful listening and talking? Check out this dialogue between a mother and son.

Mom: How many times do I have to ask you to clean up after you have your snack?

Son: I hear you, Mom.

Mom: Then stop watching TV and put your dishes away. At least clean up after yourself. I can't be responsible for everything in this house.

Son: I'm listening, Mom. I'm wondering if it would be okay if I watched the last five minutes of my show and then cleaned up.

Mom: That sounds fair. Just don't make me tell you again. By the way, what's come over you that you're not talking back like you usually do?

Son: I'm trying something new we learned at school. It has to do with Mindfulness.

Mom: How about telling me about it after dinner? I'd like to hear about it.

Son: Sure, no problem.

Here's another scene, this time played out between Sean, a twelve-year-old boy, and Chelsea, his fourteen-year-old sister. She's trying to do her homework, and he's chasing around the room after Wolf, their dog, making loud dog noises.

Chelsea: I'm trying to study for a big test tomorrow. Can't you go outside with the dog?

Sean: It's my house too. Why can't you go up to your room and study? I was here first.

Chelsea: I could go upstairs, but I like to do my work here in the family room, where it's bright and sunny. How about if I stay here for half an hour and then go upstairs? I'd appreciate it if you and Wolf would go outside until I get a little studying done, and then I'll call you when the time's up. How does that sound?

Sean: Okay, I guess. Hey, wait. Why are you being so nice?

Chelsea: No special reason, but I can understand that you like to run around and let off steam after you're cooped up in school all day. I feel the same way.

Sean: Okay. Call me in half an hour so I know when to come back in.

Chelsea: No problem.

In both of these scenes, the son in the first, and the sister in the second, used mindfulness techniques to stop a problem before it started. They listened, and they spoke kindly and respectfully. They got the results they wanted, and the other person felt satisfied with the outcome too. Think about using Mindfulness if you want to enjoy more peaceful relationships with your family.

TRY IT OUT

Think about the Hardest Part of Family Communication

Answer these questions in your Mindfulness Journal: When you and a family member are having a disagreement, which do you think is most difficult, talking or listening? Explain why you feel that way. What can you do to improve your talking or listening skills when dealing with family members? Write down your ideas, and talk about them in a class discussion.

List Helpful Ways You Can Talk and Listen to Your Family

In your Mindfulness Journal, list three ways you can talk and listen mindfully to your family members to scale back on arguments. What would help you have better communication? Use these techniques when you do the next activity.

Try Mindful Talking and Listening with Your Family

For two or three days, try mindful talking and listening with one person in your family with whom you often disagree, such as a parent, brother, or sister. Write a few sentences in your Mindfulness Journal telling how your communication was different from the way it usually is. Discuss your experiment with your small group. A chairperson from each group summarizes for the class how things worked out with group members when they talked and listened mindfully.

Role-Play a Family Scene the Mindful Way

With your group, role-play a scene using mindful talking and listening with a family member or members, and act it out for the class. Use an actual experience you've had, or use one of the examples below. After the role-plays, the class discusses what they learned from watching the scenes.

Sample Scenes

- Your mother tells you to take the dog outside, and you're watching your favorite show.
- Your dad tells you if you get less than a B average you're grounded.
- Your brother wants to eat the last piece of cake you've been saving for yourself.

MINI MEDITATION

Breathe in and out slowly twice. Let any tension you're feeling leave your body as you breathe deeply in and out. Imagine what it would be like to use mindfulness techniques with your parents, siblings, or other family members. Picture yourself and a specific relative, one with whom you sometimes disagree, speaking kindly and respectfully to one another. *I am using* I *messages and making my words positive even when I don't agree with what my family member is saying, even if I'm feeling angry or upset. I choose to take the high road and make the first move to listen by putting myself in the other person's shoes. I will use mindful talking and listening with the belief that it will make my life and my family's life happier and more peaceful.*

Chapter Twelve

Be Present in School

BE PRESENT

In addition to being present to your family and friends, you'll want to be present in your classes in school. Being in the moment in your classes will help you get better grades and will also boost your interest in what you're learning, making school a more pleasurable experience. Of course, it's easy to be in the moment and show your full attention when you're learning about a subject you like.

What about a subject that doesn't grab your attention, a subject that isn't one of your favorites? It's definitely not as easy to pay attention when the subject doesn't appeal to you. However, if you tune in to the subject mindfully, even when you're tempted to tune out, you may find that learning about a subject you're not enthusiastic about can still be a good experience.

As you know, Mindfulness asks us to be curious about everything. Try applying this curiosity to a subject you don't like by focusing on an aspect of the subject you find even slightly interesting, and think about how you could learn even more if you opened your mind to all parts of the subject. If you're open to learning any subject and give it a fair chance, you'll find it more enjoyable.

Focus mindfully on what you're learning, and if you don't understand something, be curious. Ask your teacher and a classmate who likes the subject questions until you understand it better. If you're still having trouble, request a conference and ask the teacher to explain what's giving you trouble in a way you can better understand it. We all have different learning styles, and when we get information in our own personal learning style, we understand it much better. You just have to find out what your individual learning style is.

Some kids learn best by seeing (visual learners), some by hearing (auditory learners), and some by getting hands-on experiences (kinesthetic learners). Think about which method helped you to learn best in the past, especially with a subject that challenged you. Ask the teacher to explain things to fit the way you learn best. Later in this chapter, you'll find an explanation of learning styles that will help you determine what yours is.

Homework is another part of school that often boggles kids' minds. After you sit in school all day, you're asked to boost the skills you've learned by reading, solving problems, and figuring out answers to questions that may be so hard you wonder if even the teacher knows them. Look at it this way: homework can be something you barely tolerate, something you dread, or a positive experience you can use to boost what you've learned in school.

Think about how you'd like to approach doing homework. Even though it's not your choice about doing homework, you can choose how you'll think about it. If you see it as something you dislike and something you want to get over with fast so you can do your own thing, then you'll probably find it an unpleasant experience. However, if you look at it as a way to help you understand what you've learned in your classes and you have an open mind when you sit down to do it, you'll be a step ahead. You'll do better in your tests and probably see your grades improve because you were mindful when you did your homework.

Test taking is another aspect of school many kids dread. You already know that when you're stressed before you take a test, you probably won't do your best. Although a normal amount of stress can help you perform, too much stress can work the opposite way. If you tune in to the test by making an effort to understand each step of the question, you'll have a better chance of coming up with the right answer. If you get stuck, move on to another question, and save the ones that stumped you for later.

TRY IT OUT

Be Curious about a Class

The next time you sit in a class that doesn't interest you, try being curious and ask yourself questions like: How can this subject help me? Why do other kids like it? (Ask some of them who do.) What can I find in this subject that might interest me? After you try this mindfulness technique, answer the questions above in your Mindfulness Journal to determine how your curiosity helped you view the subject in a different way. Discuss with the class and compare notes.

Target Your Learning Style

When you want to understand a school subject better, it may help to consider how you learn best. Once you figure out your individual learning style, ask the teacher of a subject you don't particularly like to explain the work to you in your own personal learning style. Do you learn best by seeing, hearing, or by having hands-on experiences? Tune into your best learning style, and see if it helps you gain a new appreciation for all your subjects, even those you don't like.

After reading about the types of learning styles, write what you think your learning style is and explain why you think so. If you think you have a combination of learning styles, state what you think they are, and list them in your Mindfulness Journal. See the chart below that explains the three major types of learning styles. If you're not sure about which learning style helps you learn best, see what your counselor or teacher thinks, based on what you tell them.

Types of Learning Styles

Visual

If you're a visual learner, you learn best by seeing the information. Reading information from books or the Internet and seeing colors, charts, graphs, videos, and slideshows can help you learn better. Highlighter pens of different colors can help when you're reviewing your notes for a test.

Auditory

If you're an auditory learner, you learn best by hearing the information. It helps to study with a friend so you can talk about the information while hearing it. It also helps to say the information you need to remember aloud to yourself several times or to tape it.

Kinesthetic

If you're a kinesthetic learner, you learn best by hands-on experiences such as studying with other kids, role-playing, and using flash cards.

Figure Out Your Learning Style

In your Mindfulness Journal, write what you think your main learning style is and why you think so. If you think it's a combination of learning styles, explain which ones and why you think so. Discuss with the class how using this information about your learning style can help you do better in school.

You can also talk about a personal experience you had with learning better by using a certain learning style or styles.

Brainstorm Ways to Make Homework Easier

With your small group, brainstorm four tips for making homework less of a chore. Each group will compile at least three tips about being mindful when doing homework. Share your group's best tips with the class. Write down the ones other groups suggest that appeal to you, and try them the next time you do homework.

Sample Answers

- Do your most challenging subject first.
- When you do homework, be mindful by giving it your full attention. You'll get it done faster and more efficiently if you think of what you're writing, computing, or problem solving as you're doing it.
- If you have trouble with homework in a certain subject, talk it over with a friend. Help her with a subject she finds hard.
- After finishing your homework, reward yourself by doing something you enjoy.

Take Tests with Ease

In a class discussion, share your best ideas for taking tests mindfully. Use the ones you like best the next time you take a test.

Sample Answers

- Use your individual learning style or styles to help you prepare for a test.
- If you get nervous before taking a test, acknowledge and accept the discomfort. Stay with it even if you don't like the feeling. It will pass, and when it does, you can start focusing on the questions.
- Tune in to the test question before you answer. Be curious about the question. What is the question asking you? If you're taking an essay test, use scrap paper to make a brief word or phrase outline before you write. This is an outline where you use groups of words instead of complete sentences. It will help you organize your answer better. After you write, leave a few minutes to proofread for spelling and grammar errors.
- Motivate yourself to do your best on the test by using self-talk: for example, *I'm feeling a little nervous, but I can do this. I'm prepared for this test. I can work on the answers I know and go back to the harder ones later. I'm confident I'll do well.*

MINI MEDITATION

Take two deep breaths. Breathe in and out, totally calming your body and mind. Imagine how being present in school for all your subjects can help you learn better and get the grades you want. *I am curious about all my subjects, even the ones that don't excite me. I bring my understanding of Mindfulness to homework by thinking of it as more of a challenge than a chore. When taking a test, I use the techniques I've learned to tune in to the questions and come up with the best answers. School is more fun and less stressful when I use Mindfulness to help me learn.*

Chapter Thirteen

Live in Harmony with Classmates

BE PRESENT

Spending time with classmates is another important part of your school experience. You help each other grow in knowledge and in getting along with others by participating in your classes and in school activities like sports. Often your classmates become your friends.

Some of the friendships you make in elementary and middle school last into high school and possibly beyond. If you find it hard to make friends, join a school activity or club that includes kids that have similar interests as yours, such as sports, band, drama, or chorus.

If you show interest in others, they're likely to show interest in becoming your friend. If you're talking to a friend you already have, or to one you'd like to have, Mindfulness can help you communicate with him in the best way possible.

To make lasting friendships and find new ones, practice mindful talking and listening; be positive when you speak; be curious about what your friend says by asking questions; accept what your friend says even if you don't always agree; use *I* messages; and put yourself in her shoes. The most important thing is to be there for your friend. Using these mindfulness techniques helps you cement old friendships and build new ones.

It's easy to live in harmony with the kids at school who share your interests and opinions, but sometimes, even then, you may have disagreements. If you disagree with your classmate, mindfulness will often give you a helpful way to deal with it. Listen to what your friend says, and respond in a caring way without reacting. You can say something like "I don't see it the way you do, but that's okay. I know people have different ideas about things, and I respect that." Be curious and ask questions so you can better understand your classmate's point of view. Accept what he says without judging.

What if the worst happens? A classmate who doesn't see things your way tries to bully you, and you've done what you could to make her stop. If bullying continues or gets worse, talk to a trusted adult, such as a family member, teacher, counselor, or principal, and discuss how you can work together to stop the person from bothering you.

A team approach helps better than trying to deal with a tough problem like bullying without help. Sometimes it's difficult to tell an adult what's on your mind about bullying or any other serious problem. If this happens, remember to use your assertive speaking skills to say exactly what's going on and to ask for help to make things better.

Suppose you see a bully bothering another classmate. Think about standing up for the bullied child with a group of your friends and telling the bully to stop. However, if the bullying is serious or continues, you and your friends can report in private what you witnessed to a teacher or counselor.

TRY IT OUT

Make New Friends and Treasure Old Friendships

You probably have some friends you've had since you started school. These are the people you turn to if you need to talk and who turn to you if something is on their minds. If you'd like to add more kids to your circle of friends, you'll easily attract them if you practice the principles of Mindfulness.

One way to make new friends and nourish your friendships with ones you already have is to show you're truly interested in what they have to say, whether you agree with them or not. The most important thing is to be there for your friends, as you would want them to be there for you.

Tune in to what your friend is saying, and give an old friend or new one your full attention. Use all of the ideas in this book that you'll find reviewed in the "Be Present" section of this chapter to build great and lasting friendships. Kids that have a circle of true friends don't always wear the nicest clothes, look the most attractive, get the highest grades, or excel in sports. Often, they're kids who care enough to be good listeners and to put themselves in the other person's situation.

In a class discussion, talk about ways you can be a true friend to the friends you already have and also meet and make some new friends. How can being mindful help you keep old friendships and build new ones?

Be a Mindful Friend

With a partner, role-play talking and listening to a classmate/friend using the mindfulness techniques listed in the "Be Present" section. Use your own topic or see the ones below for ideas.

- A friend has trouble in English class and you're good at the subject. What can you do to help her?
- A classmate's pet died and he's very sad. What will you say to him?
- A friend tells you her parents are getting a divorce and she's upset. What can you say to help her?

Disagree the Mindful Way

You and your friend have a different opinion about something that both of you feel strongly about. What can you say to let him know you're still friends even though you have very different ideas? Think about it for a few minutes, and in your Mindfulness Journal, write a positive way to express your feelings. Share your answers with the entire class.

Use Mindful Speaking to Help a Bullied Classmate

If you see a classmate being bullied, you wonder if you should say something to the bully or tell a teacher or counselor instead. One thing you have to consider is how dangerous you think the bully is. If you think the bully might harm you, tell a responsible adult at school right away.

However, if you think you can help by saying something to the bully, be assertive in your speech and body language. Don't talk a lot; instead, use short sentences like "Don't do that," or "Stop bothering her." Better yet, gather a couple of kids you think would support you and stand with you to help your bullied classmate.

In your small group, come up with a suggestion about how to help someone you see being bullied. How would you (and your friends) use assertive language in talking to the bully to help that person? What kind of things would you say to help a classmate cope with bullying using mindfulness techniques for speaking and listening? Share your ideas with the entire class.

MINI MEDITATION

Find a comfortable position, and take two deep breaths. Let your muscles loosen until you feel completely calm. Think about how Mindfulness can help you connect with classmates and make new friends. *Mindfulness can help me be a friend who is willing to listen and understand, even when someone else's ideas are different from mine. Mindfulness helps me be there for my friends when they need someone to listen. If I disagree with a friend, the tips I've learned and practiced for speaking and listening can help. Even if I think differently, I'll be more willing to tune in and listen to what a friend is saying. I think about using Mindfulness when I want to be a good friend.*

Chapter Fourteen

Tune Down Your Sensitivity Button

BE PRESENT

Being sensitive can be a good thing if you don't let yourself get carried away. If you're sensitive, you probably feel more in touch with life. That means you experience things more deeply than some other people. Colors appear more vivid; emotions run at a higher pitch. Your sensitivity helps you enjoy nature and the people and places around you in a way that others who are less sensitive than you may not experience. You're also able to tune in to people so that you can often feel what they're feeling. You can sometimes get a vibe about what's on their minds before they even say anything.

As you probably know, sensitivity can also have a downside. You may recognize that you're hurt more easily and find it difficult to shake things off, like anger or criticism from your friends and family. If you're sensitive, you may sometimes think people are ignoring you or acting mean toward you when they didn't have that intention. You may get these impressions by viewing people's body language or by listening to the tone of their voice. Sometimes your impressions may be right, but other times they may be off the mark because your sensitivity button may kick in too forcefully.

The same mindfulness techniques that help you live in the moment help you tune down your sensitivity button so your sensitivity helps you rather than causes you problems. One thing you can do before you assume someone is ignoring you or is angry with you is take a couple of deep breaths and pause. Take the time to stop and think for a moment. Is it possible that your friend or family member is thinking of a problem he has and is trying to figure out a way to solve it? He could be caught up in his own thoughts that have nothing to do with you.

Maybe you thought a classmate you've known for a long time ignored you in the hallway on your way to class. Instead of assuming she doesn't want to be friends any more, stop for a moment. Don't assume anything. Instead, use self-talk and say to yourself that maybe she didn't see you because she was thinking about the test coming up next period or rushing to class so she wouldn't get in trouble for being late.

However, sometimes your impression that someone is angry with you may be right. If you're feeling hurt or upset about what you think is some-one's reaction or lack of reaction to you, check in with him and tune in to what he's saying. If you strongly think your friend sounds angry or impa-tient, you could say something like this, using *I* messages: "Can we talk about why I felt you seemed annoyed with me the other day? I felt hurt when I saw you in the hall and you kept on walking, and I wondered if I'd done something to upset you." If your friend is ignoring you or acting angry, ask why. If he says he's upset with you about something, discuss it without judging or getting angry yourself.

Here's the bottom line: Before activating your sensitivity button, use these mindfulness techniques: Pause, stop, and think before magnifying the situation in your mind. On the other hand, if your instincts tell you your friend is angry or ignoring you, take a minute to check in with the person who caused you to think something was wrong.

TRY IT OUT

Discuss with the Entire Class

Think of a time when your sensitivity helped you appreciate a moment in your life. How did it make your experience better? Discuss with the entire class. On the other hand, remember a time when being too sensitive caused you to misunderstand a friend or family member's actions, and discuss with the class. How can you use Mindfulness to help a situation like this? Share your ideas with the class.

Write a Self-Talk Script about a Friend Ignoring You

In your Mindfulness Journal, write three or four sentences you would say in response to this scene: Your friend passes you in the hall and doesn't greet you as he usually does. He looks down and doesn't say anything. Discuss and compare notes with the class.

Role-Play a Situation That Pushes Your Sensitivity Button

With a partner, use mindfulness techniques to role-play ideas about how you can keep calm when you think someone is angry with you or ignoring you. Think of your own situation or use one of these:

- You're doing a group project at school, and a student in the group doesn't like your ideas. He's acting more annoyed than you think he should be under the circumstances. You're wondering what brought this on.
- Your friend of many years did not invite you to a party and invited a few of your mutual friends. Why would she do this after you've been friends for so long?
- Your brother isn't talking to you much lately and you don't know why. You're wondering if he's in a bad mood about something that doesn't have anything to do with you, or if he's angry with you.

MINI MEDITATION

Take two deep breaths. Breathe in and out and let go of any stress and tension you're feeling in this moment. Imagine a time you thought someone was ignoring you or you thought your friend was upset with you. Say these words: *The next time I feel overly sensitive about the way I think someone I care about is treating me, I'll pause for a moment and ground myself in the present. I'll acknowledge the possibly that how the person acted may have nothing to do with me at all. If I feel strongly that it did, I'll discuss it with my friend and ask questions so I can better understand what's going on. When my sensitivity button is set on high, I can help myself by using Mindfulness.*

Chapter Fifteen

Deal with Disappointment

BE PRESENT

You didn't make the team, and you had counted on it. You got a poor grade on a test and didn't expect it. Your mom wouldn't let you go to your friend's house because you did something, like talking back, to annoy her. All kids face disappointments, both big and small. What matters is how you handle them. Mindfulness can help.

When you're disappointed about something, tune in to it instead of avoiding the feeling. Own up to how you're feeling by finding a way to describe it in your mind or on paper. Here are a couple of examples that show how you can describe your feelings of disappointment: "I was counting on making the team; most of my friends did," or "I was looking forward to going to my friend's house. Why did Mom have to ruin it just because I talked back? Sometimes I can't control my temper. I wish she'd understand that and know I don't always mean what I say when I'm in a bad mood."

Once you acknowledge how you feel, it can help if you tune in to your feelings about it. Eventually, it will send you on the path to acceptance even though you may not be able to do much to change what happened.

Remember that acceptance doesn't mean you have to agree with something. It means you're okay with it even though you may not like what happened. It also implies you're not going to waste time making yourself unhappy by thinking about it too much.

When you're disappointed about something, self-talk can help. Talk to yourself in your mind as you would to a friend. For example, if not making the team disappoints you, you might say, "I wanted to be on that team, but I can always try out for another sport, or I can try again next season."

If you're disappointed because you're not allowed to go to the party, your self-talk may sound something like this: "I probably should have talked to Mom in a nicer way, especially after all she does for me. I wanted to go to my friend's house. We had a lot of stuff planned, but this wouldn't have happened if I hadn't talked to Mom that way. I know I'm pretty good about showing respect most of the time, but sometimes I forget. I'll do better next time."

It's important to remember that Mindfulness tells us not to judge ourselves. Sometimes things don't work out the way we want, and that's just the way it is. We don't always have a say over what happens, as in the case of the sports team. Maybe you tried your best, but it didn't work out for some reason you couldn't control.

On the other hand, sometimes we do have control over something that disappoints us, as in the example of not being able to go to a friend's house because of talking back to your mom. In that case, you can change the way you react to find a better outcome next time. Acknowledge your mistake, resolve to do better next time, and move on.

Another important principle of Mindfulness asks you to respond rather than react to stress. Disappointments usually make us stressful, so we can think about using self-talk and not judging ourselves when we respond to stress. Doing these things will help stop the cycle of disappointment and the hurt that often goes along with it.

You've probably noticed that the more you think about how disappointed you feel about something, the more it prevents you from enjoying the present moment. You're living in the past instead of the present, and you may also be thinking about the future, wondering if you'll make the team next season, or if you'll be able to go to your friend's house next time.

Being in the present is always a better way to go because if you're living in "the now," disappointments won't bother you as much. There's always a new day and a new chance for a fresh start.

TRY IT OUT

Write about a Time You Felt Disappointed

In your Mindfulness Journal, write about a time you felt disappointed about something that happened at home or in school. How did you deal with it? If you had to go through it again, how would you use Mindfulness to help you cope? Discuss with the entire class.

Brainstorm Ideas to Help Kids Deal with Disappointment

With your group, list some disappointments you or other kids you know have faced. List the disappointments, and suggest ideas that can help kids cope with each one. Use some mindfulness ideas you've studied that can help. Discuss with the entire class.

Write a Skit about How to Deal with Disappointment

With your group, create a skit about one student's experience dealing with disappointment. Act out the skit for the class. Show how the student used Mindfulness to overcome disappointment about something that happened. Think of your own ideas or use one of the ones listed below.

- You've studied hard for a test, but on the day of the test you get nervous and can't remember a lot of what you've learned. As a result, you don't get the grade you wanted.
- Your parents finally say you can get a pet, but at the last minute they change their minds.
- One of your closest friends tells you she wants to spend more time with other kids.
- You asked your parents for something you've wanted for a long time for your birthday, but they say it costs too much and buy you something else.

MINI MEDITATION

Take two deep breaths. Relax your body from head to toe, step by step, breathing in and out slowly. Think about a time you experienced disappointment and how you handled it. *Mindfulness can help me when I feel disappointed. I can use mindfulness techniques, like tuning in to my feelings, self-talk, and responding rather than reacting, to make disappointment less upsetting. Living in the present helps me deal with disappointment. If I take each moment as it comes and go with it without chasing it away, whether good or bad, I am living in the present. Disappointments happen to everyone. I choose not to let disappointments keep me from being happy.*

Chapter Sixteen

Stop Bad Moods Quickly

BE PRESENT

Bad moods can drag you down fast and can come on when you least expect them. But like dealing with disappointments, Mindfulness can help you keep bad moods away or at least to a minimum.

Sometimes the slightest thing can send you into a bad mood. You and your friend have been having a lot of disagreements lately; your mom bugs you about something that wasn't your fault; or your teacher criticizes you. When something like this happens, you may give in to your bad mood and let it take over how you feel for most of the day. Who would blame you if you snapped back or got disgusted and walked away from the person or situation? After all, it's usually another person or situation that puts you in a bad mood. Or is it?

Often the way you react to what someone says or what happens to you can change your mood from happy and upbeat to angry or irritable. But think about this: It's up to you how you respond.

You have another choice if you think about using Mindfulness to nudge you out of your bad mood. The first thing you can do is stop, take a couple of deep breaths, and pause. Is what happened worth making yourself unhappy and irritable? Next, tune in to how you feel about it. Stay with the feeling, and be curious. Think about how your mind and body are starting to react to whatever upset you. Remember that you have the choice of staying calm and steady so you can enjoy your day or falling into a dark, dismal mood that prevents you from having fun.

After you think about how you're feeling in your mind and body (e.g., angry, upset, sweaty hands, and muscle tightness), acknowledge and accept your symptoms even if they're unpleasant. Let go of them in your own time, but make that a reasonable amount of time. You definitely don't want to spend the day being unhappy or not enjoying doing the things you love.

The next step is to talk to the person involved about the situation that set off your bad mood. Use assertive communication that doesn't cause blame or anger. *I* messages help get your point across without making the other person angry or upset. Stay positive when you talk, and be sure to listen to the person you're talking to without judging. It's up to you to choose to give in to a bad mood or to let a good mood take over. Sure, some things can put you in a bad mood, but you can decide how long you want to hold on to it. You can decide to live in the present, to enjoy every moment rather than waste time thinking about something that probably wasn't that important anyway. If you're mindful of your moods, you can bounce back more quickly from a bad mood. Why not give it a try?

TRY IT OUT

Write about a Time a Bad Mood Took Over

In your Mindfulness Journal, write about something or someone that put you in a bad mood. How did you handle it? Now that you know about Mindfulness, how would you have handled the situation differently? Discuss with the entire class.

Role-Play Using Mindfulness to Improve a Bad Mood

With a partner, role-play a scene showing what put you in a bad mood and how you used one or more mindfulness techniques to get you out of it. Write two scenes, one in which you are in a bad mood, and one in which your partner is in one. The class will comment on how the techniques you used worked and give their own ideas. Use your own ideas or one of the topics below to write your scene.

- The coach didn't choose you for the team, but your best friend made it.
- Your dad says you have to visit a relative with the family, and you've already made plans with your friends to go to a movie.
- Your friend starts an argument over something you don't consider important.

Write Self-Talk for Dealing with a Bad Mood

In your Mindfulness Journal, write some helpful things to say to yourself if you find yourself in a bad mood. First, name the situation that put you in a bad mood. If you can't think of one, make one up. Then write a few things you'd say to yourself to help. Discuss your ideas with a partner, and ask each other if you would add any other suggestions. Share your ideas with the class.

MINI MEDITATION

Breathe in and out slowly twice. Think of how happy and upbeat you feel when you're in a good mood. Imagine how light and laid-back you feel and how peaceful your mind is. *I'm thinking about the kinds of things I can do to put myself in a good mood. I'm remembering the last time I felt in a great mood. I'm thinking of the way my body and mind felt and why I loved feeling this way. I'm deciding to shake off bad moods more quickly when they come along. Mindfulness helps me look on the bright side when things happen that make me want to give in to anger. It's my choice not to let a bad mood drag me down.*

Chapter Seventeen

Cope with Frustration Now

BE PRESENT

Being frustrated about something can tie you up in knots. You want so badly to be able to do something like understand a school subject better, but it isn't happening. Maybe your parent tells you that you can't do something you've been looking forward to like going to a friend's for a sleepover or that you can't have something you want badly like a new electronic device. Sometimes frustration sets in when someone criticizes you for something you think is unfair. Whatever the reason for your frustration, it's a feeling everyone experiences at one time or another.

Just as Mindfulness can help you with other problems you face, it can boost your power to deal with any frustrations that come your way. Think of it this way. Mindfulness can act as a buffer for all the feelings that come with frustration, such as anger, sadness, annoyance, and a sense of helplessness.

When you're feeling frustrated, stop and pause for a moment. Tune in to sensations in your body like tightness or tension in your muscles. Maybe you feel nervous and upset and don't know what to do to get rid of these unpleasant feelings. Don't push them away. Instead, allow yourself to experience them. Then use self-talk to work through the situation.

You can also find a friend or family member who is a good listener to talk about your feelings of frustration. Listen to their suggestions, but in the end, you'll be the one to decide how to deal with what upset and frustrated you. Trust your judgment. That is another principle of Mindfulness. Even if you make a mistake, it will be okay. You can always rethink your plan of action and try something else if your first idea doesn't work to your satisfaction.

You don't have to stay stuck in frustration and all the unpleasant feelings that go with it if you go with your feelings, own up to them and accept them, and then look for a solution. You can leave frustration behind and figure out how to work with it to find a good solution.

TRY IT OUT

Brainstorm Some Things That Cause Kids Frustration

Meet with your small group and brainstorm some issues that cause kids frustration. Map out a plan for dealing with five of these frustrations with mindfulness techniques. Discuss your ideas with the entire class.

What Can You Do When Someone Says No to Something You Want?

Think of a time when someone said *no* to something you wanted. List the steps you would take to help you cope with it using mindfulness techniques. Exchange your ideas with a partner and listen mindfully to each other's responses. Discuss your ideas with the class.

Role-Play a Scene That Tells How You Can Deal with Frustration Mindfully

With a partner, talk about something that frustrates you. Next, show how you can use one or more mindfulness techniques, such as acknowledging your feelings and using self-talk, to deal with what happened. Then explain how you would confide in a friend or family member about what frustrates you. Share your ideas in a class discussion.

   Use your own idea or one of these:

- Your parent makes negative comments about what you're wearing
- You want to spend all your holiday money, but your parents insist you save half of it.
- You find it hard to keep up with the other kids in gym class.

MINI MEDITATION

Take two deep, cleansing breaths. Bring a feeling of restfulness to your mind and body. Think of a time when you were frustrated by something you found difficult to do, when someone criticized you, or when someone said *no* to you about something you thought was important.

When I feel frustrated, I tune in to my physical and emotional sensations. I acknowledge the feelings and accept them, whatever they are. They cannot control me unless I give them permission. I decide which mindfulness techniques I'll use to deal with feelings of frustration. I always have control of how I respond to my feelings of frustration and to any other negative feelings that come my way.

Chapter Eighteen

Tame Your Anger

BE PRESENT

Think of how many times you can become angry during the course of a day. Sometimes it's little things, such as not being able to find your report for school or big things, such as a kid on your bus pushing you for no reason. Like frustration, anger can make you feel bad physically and emotionally. In fact, it can push your buttons worse than frustration. That's why learning to control your anger will help you enjoy life more. You can't have fun when anger invades your life like a wild beast. It's hard to concentrate in school or enjoy activities with your friends.

Just as practicing Mindfulness helps you with tuning down your sensitivity button, dealing with disappointment, stopping bad moods, and coping with frustration, it can also help you manage anger. When you get angry, practicing Mindfulness can make anger disappear more quickly so you don't have to carry it around with you for a long time.

One thing that can definitely help you with anger, in addition to using mindfulness techniques, is practicing a form of meditation every day for at least ten or fifteen minutes. You can sit in a chair or sit cross-legged on a big cushion on the floor. Try different types of meditation to see which one you like best.

You can meditate by being aware of your breath. Be aware of when you're breathing in and when you're breathing out. Whenever thoughts come into your mind, go back to your breath. Keep a clock nearby so you can peek at it every so often as your meditation time comes to a close. As the time draws near to stop meditating, gently open your eyes and stretch your arms and legs. Come out of your meditation gradually.

Another type of meditation you can do to help you keep calm is called mantra meditation. To do this, you'll think a word in your mind instead of concentrating on your breath. It can be any word you want, like *peace, flower*, or *relax*. It can even be a word you make up. The word itself doesn't matter because it's a tool to help you relax. Every time other thoughts enter your mind, come back to your special word. When your meditation's over, come out of it gradually as you did with the meditation where you used your breath to focus.

When you meditate, be sure you won't be distracted by anyone or by loud noises. Tell the people in your house you're going to meditate and to please not disturb you.

In addition to adding meditation to your daily routine, you can practice mindfulness techniques to help curb anger. First, stop and pause. Tune in to your feelings of anger and stay with them. Be aware of what's happening in your body, like breathing faster and perspiring, and in your mind, like feeling sad or stressful.

Next, acknowledge and accept your feelings about anger. That doesn't mean you agree with what happened to make you angry. Experience your feelings of anger and accept that they're happening. Then gradually decide to let go of as much of the anger as you can. If you feel someone made you angry, talk calmly to the person involved using *I* messages. Be positive and listen to what the other person has to say. In the case of a person who would harm you physically or emotionally, bypass that person and talk to an adult you trust, who will advise you about the bullying. It isn't easy dealing with your feelings of anger, but Mindfulness can help.

TRY IT OUT

Create a Poster Showing How Anger Makes You Feel

With your group, create a poster showing how anger can make you feel. Use a large poster board and different colored markers. Use adjectives to show the physical and emotional things that can happen when anger strikes. Draw pictures or cartoon figures on the poster to show how kids feel when they're angry. If you want, cut and paste pictures from magazines. Make your poster as bright and inviting as possible. One person from the group can explain your poster to the class.

With Your Group, Role-Play a Situation That Made You Angry

Think of a situation that made you angry, or make one up. Your group will role-play this situation for the class and show how you'd use mindfulness techniques to help get rid of your anger. One person in the group can act as the discussion leader after your group performs the role-play for the class.

Write a Script Showing How Self-Talk Can Help You Deal with Anger

Each person in your small group writes a script showing how self-talk can help with anger. Share your ideas with one person in the group and discuss them. The person who looks at your ideas can add suggestions. Strive to make each other's scripts even better. The group chooses one script to read to the class after reading all the scripts. When reading your script to the class, first tell what the situation is and then present the script. Use your own situation for the script, or use one of the ones below:

- Your parents promised you and your friend a trip to the amusement park, and now they say they're too busy to go.
- Your teacher accuses you of looking at your friend's paper during a test, and you didn't do it.
- Your friend says mean things to you.
- Your brother calls you a terrible name.

MINI MEDITATION

Take two deep breaths, breathing in and out slowly. Let go of any tension that you feel in your body and mind. Imagine a time when you felt perfectly contented and relaxed. Think about how your body and your mind felt. *When I use Mindfulness to curb my anger, I feel happy, free, and filled with positive energy, the opposite of how I feel when I'm angry. If I meditate every day and use mindfulness techniques, I can lessen the effects of anger on my body and my mind. If I make the effort to let my anger go instead of holding on to it, I'll feel happy, free, and filled with the best kind of energy every day. I'll live in the present in the best way possible.*

Chapter Nineteen

Practice Loving Kindness

BE PRESENT

Mindfulness teaches us to be kind to ourselves and others. Some people who practice Mindfulness call it *loving kindness*. Just so you know, loving kindness is not an overdone, mushy way of thinking or a fake attempt to be extra nice to people. Rather, it's a sincere willingness to act caring with yourself and others and to give yourself and those you come in contact with the benefit of the doubt even when it's hard.

Loving kindness means going out of your way to help others when they're hurting in some way or when you see they need someone to care. Do you remember when we discussed putting yourself in another's shoes? To show loving kindness and compassion, a caring attitude toward others, you have to be able to feel what they're feeling and think like they're thinking.

Loving kindness also means giving yourself a little slack when you think you've messed up in some way. It means treating yourself kindly and gently rather than putting yourself down for the same mistakes a lot of other people make. This mindful way of looking at things gives you the ability to forgive yourself and move on.

What kinds of things can you do to show loving kindness to yourself besides not being too hard on yourself when you make a mistake? You can allow yourself to be who you are and not be terribly disappointed if you don't achieve what you see as perfection in school, sports, or your social life. You can forgive yourself if you do something you regret and then move on and start fresh. You'll be better able to keep your cool even when things aren't going your way because you know that better days will follow.

How can you show loving kindness to your family and friends? You can be there for them when they need you and show them in small ways how much you care about them. It's often the small things you do for people that they remember the most. Let them know how important they are to you by your words and actions. Every so often, make them feel appreciated by helping them without waiting for them to ask or spending quality time with them without electronic distractions.

Loving kindness sets Mindfulness into action because it's a way of showing you care about yourself and the people in your life.

TRY IT OUT

List Three Ways to Show Loving Kindness

In your group, brainstorm three ways you can show loving kindness to family and friends. Share your ideas in a class discussion. In the next few weeks, try some of the ideas your classmates suggested. Write about the one you did that you liked best in your Mindfulness Journal.

Examples of Loving Kindness toward Others

- Your friend tried out for the basketball and didn't make it. Talk to her in a kind way and help her feel better.
- Your mom feels exhausted when she gets home from work. Offer to help her with dinner or cleaning up.
- Your grandfather doesn't look as happy as he usually does. Cheer him up by taking a walk with him or having dessert together.

Think of Ways You Can Show Yourself Loving Kindness

In your Mindfulness Journal, list two situations that call for loving kindness involving yourself, and using these situations, write two ways you can show yourself loving kindness. See the examples below for ideas. Share your answers in a class discussion.

Examples of Loving Kindness toward Yourself

- You didn't get the report card you expected. Console yourself with self-talk like this: "I did my best, so it's no big deal. Next time will probably be better."
- You had a major disagreement with your best friend, and you said things you regret. Now you're feeling embarrassed. What could you say to yourself to show loving kindness? What could you say to your friend?

Write a Short Poem That Shows Loving Kindness toward Yourself or Others

Write a four- to six-line free verse poem about showing loving kindness.

Example of a Poem about Loving Kindness for Yourself

> May I enjoy every moment by living in the present.
> May I be able to handle anything
> that comes my way calmly and peacefully,
> even when it's not easy.
> May I feel be safe, strong, and healthy
> so I can live the best life ever.

Example of a Poem That Shows Loving Kindness toward Others

> May you feel peaceful and joyful
> and do what makes you happy.
> May you enjoy the warmth of friendships
> and closeness with those you care about.
> May you be strong, healthy, and
> shine brightly in everything you do.

Volunteers read their poems to the class. Write or print your poem neatly, and mount it on construction paper. Illustrate your poem with your own drawings or with pictures you cut from magazines. Your teacher will display poems in the classroom and hallways.

Brainstorm Ways to Show Loving Kindness

With your group, brainstorm three ways of showing loving kindness to yourselves and three ways of showing it to others. Present your best ideas to the class. After all groups give their tips for showing loving kindness, choose your favorite one for showing loving kindness to yourself or to others. Make it a point to practice loving kindness in this way. On a day the teacher chooses, volunteers report back to the class about how their experiment with loving kindness worked for them. Here are some examples to give you ideas.

Show Loving Kindness to Yourself

- The next time something goes wrong, don't be too hard on yourself. Give yourself credit for all the good things you've done. Pamper yourself by doing something you enjoy. Give yourself a little reward for being you.
- You've had a bad day so far, and things aren't going your way. Try to get away from what's upsetting you. Go outside and enjoy nature. Pet an

animal. Talk to a friend. Treat yourself kindly. Tell yourself that this too shall pass.

Show Loving Kindness to Others

• Your mom had a hard day at work. Think of what you can do to help her feel better. Fix dinner, clean up, or show her some extra kindness.
• Your friend fell and hurt his leg. Bring him a special treat to cheer him up. Spend some time with him talking on the phone or visiting.

MINI MEDITATION

Take a few deep breaths until your body feels completely rested. Think about a time you showed loving kindness to yourself and how it made you feel. Remember a time you showed loving kindness to another person and how it made a difference in that person's life. *Showing loving kindness to myself and others can make my life more peaceful and happy. I wish only the best for myself and those I care about. I wish myself and others good health, happiness, and the joy of living every moment and making each moment count. May I show loving kindness to myself and others every day.*

Chapter Twenty

Whatever Is, Is—and That's Okay

BE PRESENT

By now, you've learned that Mindfulness can make you calmer, help you get along better with everyone, excel in school, and deal with problems that can cause you stress, like bad moods, daily frustrations, and anger.

Perhaps one of the most important things Mindfulness teaches is that you may not like some things that happen, but you can accept these things and still be okay. It's true some things that happen, like losing at a sports event or having an argument with a friend, are much less stressful than others, like getting the flu the day of the school trip or finding out your pet has a serious illness.

However, Mindfulness gives you ways of dealing with anything that happens to you in life, even the most upsetting things. To recap what you've learned, the first thing to do if something stressful happens is to pause and take a moment to think about how it's affecting you right now.

How does what took place make you feel in your body and your mind? Don't try to deny your feelings even if it causes you discomfort. Go with the sensations, whatever they are. After you have experienced them, be willing to let the discomfort go. That doesn't mean what happened hasn't affected you. It means you're going to deal with it, no matter how difficult it is, in the best possible way.

When something happens that causes you stress, you can choose how to respond, or you can react, which can make you feel worse. If you practice Mindfulness, you will eventually come to an acceptance of what has happened because Mindfulness teaches us to accept things just as they are.

Remember, there is always something you can do even if you feel you can't deal with what happened. You can use self-talk. You may want to tell

85

yourself that despite how you feel at the time, you will not always feel this way and will gradually be able to cope with whatever happened. You can also talk with a sympathetic family member, friend, or someone you trust at school like a teacher or counselor. There is always help, no matter how small or big your problem is. All you have to do is ask.

TRY IT OUT

Write about a Time You Weren't Okay with What Happened

In your Mindfulness Journal write about a time when you felt you weren't okay with what happened. How did it affect you? What mindfulness techniques would you try if it happened again? Volunteers discuss their answers with the class when the teacher asks for students to share their ideas.

Brainstorm Situations and Solutions with Your Group

With your group, brainstorm some things you've found hard to deal with. Discuss how Mindfulness can help you cope with them if you face something like that again. A member of the group can present a summary of the group's ideas to the entire class. See what other ideas the class adds to your group's suggestions for dealing with the issues your group mentioned.

Role-Play a Situation That Requires a Good Listener

Think of a situation where it would be hard for you to accept "what is." Role-play talking about it with a partner who uses mindfulness techniques, such as a positive attitude, good listening, and putting oneself in another person's shoes.

As a topic, use something you or a friend experienced, or base your role-play on one of the situations below. Act out your role-play for the class and discuss with the class how talking to someone who listens helps you deal with a difficult situation.

- You are going to visit your sick grandfather in the hospital, and he isn't doing well.
- Your family can't go on vacation this year, and you've been looking forward to it for a long time.
- You're having big problems getting along with a family member.

MINI MEDITATION

Take two deep, calming breaths. Mellow out, and just be in the moment. Think of what the phrase "whatever is, is" means to you. Are there things you would find hard to accept? Think of something that happened that you found hard to deal with. How did you respond? *If I use Mindfulness to deal with challenging issues, it can help a lot. I can start by stopping for a moment and pausing rather than reacting right away. I can use self-talk to put things in perspective and talk to a good listener who puts herself in my shoes. When I have problems I find hard to deal with, I'll remember that whatever is, is, and deal with them the best way I can. When I am faced with something that upsets me, I use mindfulness techniques to help me cope.*

Chapter Twenty-One

Be Aware of the Moment—Breathe!

BE PRESENT

As you know, being aware of your breath is an important part of Mindfulness. When you're conscious of your breathing, it grounds you in the moment. You are fully alive and aware of what's happening when you concentrate on your breath. You're living mindfully. Simply taking a couple of deep breaths can help you pause and tune in to wherever you happen to be at any moment.

Being aware of your breath can bring you back to the present when you're trying to be a good listener and when you're putting yourself in another person's shoes. It can also help when you're dealing with the frustrations and disappointments that everyone faces or when you want to change your mood from bad to good. You can cut down on stress and live in harmony with your family and classmates if you become aware of your breath before you react. Take the time to take a couple of deep breaths when you're facing a difficult situation.

Being aware of your breath can also help you tame your anger. It helps you with whatever you're trying to do, like talking to get results or doing your best in school. Thinking about your breath reminds you that whatever is, is, and that's okay. Mindfulness teaches that we can be okay with what's going on in our lives, just as it is. It suggests staying with what the moment brings, no matter what's happening.

When you use your breath to meditate, it helps bring you back to the present if your mind starts wandering. If thoughts going through your head interrupt you when you're meditating, come back to your breath. If you're using a mantra (special word) to meditate, you can also think of the word if your mind takes you on a different path. Your breath or mantra will always bring you back to the present moment.

If you're using your breath to meditate, focus on the sensation of breathing in and out. Be aware of the air coming in and out of your nostrils as you breathe. While you're meditating, be curious about the process of breathing. Give your attention to your breath whenever your mind wanders or when you become aware of other thoughts or outside noises in the room.

While you're meditating, maybe you feel the urge to scratch an annoying itch or your stomach starts growling like a bear. All you need to do is bring your attention back to the flow of your breath or the rising and falling of your chest. You'll return once again to the moment. If you want, put your hand on your chest to feel your breath moving in and out.

Whatever type of meditation you choose to do, remember to end the meditation gradually. You can do this by no longer focusing on your breath or the mantra and slowly stretching. Surprisingly, you'll find yourself refreshed, relaxed, and filled with more energy than if you had taken a long nap.

Being aware of your breath while you're going about your daily activities helps you live mindfully, and that's a great way to live every moment. Whatever you're doing and wherever you are, tune in, take a breath, and be in the moment.

TRY IT OUT

Brainstorm Ways Breathing Mindfully Can Help

With your small group, brainstorm three ways that paying attention to your breath during your daily activities can help you deal with problems. Discuss with the entire class. When you face stress of any kind in your life, take a deep breath or two, and feel your mind and body relax instantly. Try being conscious of your breathing the next time you think you need it. On a day your teacher chooses, report back to the class on how breathing mindfully worked for you.

Meditate by Using Your Breath

Find a quiet place in your home where no one will disturb you. Have a watch, Smartphone, or clock nearby so you can begin to wind down your meditation in ten or fifteen minutes. Start your meditation by breathing in and out naturally and at your own pace. When thoughts come into your mind or when you hear noises around you, simply go back to your breath and use it to bring you back to the moment.

You can close your eyes, but peek at the clock every so often when you think the time for your meditation is coming to an end. Gradually stop concentrating on your breath, stretch gently, and end your meditation. Move on to your next activity relaxed and refreshed.

Within a few minutes of stopping your meditation, write ideas in your Mindfulness Journal about how the meditation went. Did you find it a pleasant experience? Would you change anything about it next time? Would you like to make it part of your daily or weekly routine? Why or why not? If you've tried mantra meditation, which type of meditation do you prefer, using your breath or a mantra? Explain your preference. Volunteers will share answers in a class discussion.

Make a Poster about How Breathing Can Help You Become More Mindful

With your group, brainstorm ways paying attention to your breath can help you live more mindfully. Create a poster, illustrating it with pictures you draw, or cut and paste pictures from magazines. Each group can present its poster to the class.

MINI MEDITATION

Take two deep breaths, breathing in and out slowly. Think about how taking these calming breaths helps you feel free and focused. Think of a situation you've faced lately where taking a couple of deep breaths would help you consider the problem in a calm, cool way. *I think about how I feel in my body and my mind when I take a deep breath and exhale slowly. I feel more peaceful and relaxed in my mind. I notice how time seems to stand still and how whatever I'm dealing with seems less upsetting. When I take a deep breath, my body feels less stressful and more energetic. I am aware of the moment when I breathe and focus on my breath. I do my best to live mindfully every day in every way.*

www.ingramcontent.com/pod-product-compliance
Lightning Source LLC
Chambersburg PA
CBHW020358270326
41926CB00007B/487